Take Me To Your Breeder

Letters from an Extraterrestrial Anthropologist

Dust Cover

What would an extraterrestrial zoologist do upon first encountering the inhabitants of planet earth?

First, he would have to find a way to merge with a human, perhaps a long succession of humans, in order to carry out his work.

Secondly, he would have to change his title to anthropologist lest he suffer persecution at the hands of the most violent sentient beings in the galaxy!

Last, but not least, he would have to convince the humans to change their terrible ways by subtle means, for, if he fails in his mission, earth will be weaponized by hurling it at Andromeda in hopes that humanity might set that galaxy back a few eons.

Within this book the reader will find the 18 letters of Regal M-116-S to the Primates of Blue, and one lone missive to the four-legs.

Take Me To Your Breeder

Take Me To Your Breeder

For Craig Oliver Myles, one of my favorite humans, and despite that, a credit to sentient kind

Contents

Coming out of The Extraterrestrial Closet

A couple of years ago I wrote an article from the point of view of an extraterrestrial anthropologist. It was something I was writing from an apolitical perspective and I thought that my take would appear as most alien to the readers. After reading it Adam Swinder called me from Virginia and informed me that my opinion pieces were far more believable coming from the perspective of an alien than a human.

A chill struck me.

Was it alien psychology interfacing poorly with human physiology?

Was he right?

Or was I simply insane?

Until that moment I had thought that I was a politically incorrect gonzo violence author and oddball sci-fi writer pretending to write as regal M-116-S. But after Adam hung up and I felt a gurgling in my gut that might have given pause to a gastroenterologist, I knew then the truth; that James LaFond is just a mask I wear as I explore your bizarre Planet of The Apes.

Eight Years of Mighty Right

A Letter from an Extraterrestrial Anthropologist

© 2012 James LaFond

Planet Earth

The Experimental American Primate Habitat

Collection Point: Baltimore, Maryland

A Note to the 127 Sentient Inhabitants

11/12/2012

Last week I became a 'facebooker'. This resulted in two realizations on my part. First, I was required to name my hometown. Although my actual community of origin cannot be pronounced in any of your simian languages I did decide to be as truthful as I could. I listed my point of entry into your world, Machu Picchu. So the truth is out, and you ancient astronaut theorists may feel better about yourselves. I am an ancient alien; not an invader though, merely a researcher working off a grant on extinction events…

Take Me To Your Breeder

These past two weeks on facebook I have noticed much concern about the reaffirmation of your leader. There was a big fuss about his ritualized reselection. Politicians bore me, so I cannot say I remember their names. I am something of a religious buff however. I do believe one was a prominent member of a mystical Christian cult, the descendent of a very lucky prophet—archaeologically speaking that is. Your ruler's faith was also a subject of debate, and I believe You People are still in disagreement about his metaphysical loyalties.

To the extent that I 'followed' this simian chest-thumping ritual—really humans, you are no longer dwelling in the rainforest and do have interstellar aspirations. Perhaps some form of testing is in order—I noted with some dismay that the issue was not thought to have been predetermined. Your best political analysts were calling it a 'close race' up until the end. I did not even bother following the race after Sunday, knowing that You People get pretty irrational for the last two days running up to the affirmation of your autocrat.

On the night preceding your penultimate dominance ritual—I like you prizefights much more by-the-way—an Earthling friend of mine [everyone should have an Earthling friend!] warned me to stay off the street in case the ruler was not reaffirmed, as I reside among various primitives to whom he is patron. Predictably, the only thing that transpired was an orderly affirmation. I was thus spared having to chronicle the demise of this host. This is certainly not the best biomechanical observation platform I have transmigrated into. It his home though, and I have 17 more terrestrial years on my warrantee...

Since You People favor rulers who espouse contradictory ideals there never seems to be a clear majority happy with the ending. This too has its purpose. Ritual affirmation contests [elections for you ground-dwelling primates] are essentially elaborate magic tricks executed on a vast sociological scale. Unfortunately, an actual explanation of the process would violate my directive—I am slaving away beneath the weighty stipulations of a galactic grant you know—on non interference.

Let me just hit you with some raw data.

Your rulers, and institutions of rule, are the lineal descendents of patriarchal nomad horseman. Before these nomad horsemen descended from the steppes and crushed and subjected the matriarchal farming societies of the river valleys and began the primate experiment with 'civilization' there had been kings. Although your despised females actually held social power in their delicate hands they had noted the need to have a male leader; a visible pincushion for those unwashed horse-archers. Smart girls I'd say.

As, one-by-one, the female power-bases that underscored early farming societies were buried under the new male-dominated political strata, compromises were made. Female primates are cunning after all, and their conquerors were sleeping with them. Pre-conquest ritual kingships were generally terminated with the death of the king every eight years. This was retained as the Olympic cycle, which honored the king of the gods, Zeus. Eventually the cycle was halved; the occasion being so lucrative for the priesthood as to result in their doubling of production to meet demand.

This four-year cycle remains the sacral period recognized worldwide by your primate athletes— and the makers of this tasty cereal I am munching on—and by the people of your most powerful nation. Furthermore, You People have unwittingly returned to the eight-year cycle adhered to by the ancient sacral kings, by limiting the enthronement of your own king to 'two terms.'

Just as the ancient Cretans certainly cheered for their waning king as he strapped on his armored gauntlets to fight his challenger—8 years his junior, and not dissipated by as many years of limitless opium-laced wine and women—you, the descendents of their conquerors, cheer as well; but at the halfway point of his reign. In this way you may enjoy the thrill of seeing your leader struggle and not have to endure the trauma of seeing him fall. The only time a Reigning American King will be permitted to fall is when he has declined to continue as the symbolic object of your consent, or when he has disobeyed his handlers.

In the 1960s and 70s your kings all failed their handlers in one way or the other, and paid their various prices, including the most ancient one. They are thankfully now better trained*, and I believe you may enjoy many an uninterrupted eight-year reign. Do not fret; an orderly succession of kings is the hallmark of a stable matriarchal primate society. After six thousand odd years of studying you folks I'm glad to see the old girls finally make a comeback...

*On a personal note, I must confess to a nostalgic sense of loss when I observe such thoroughly domesticated figureheads, having dined with Vlad Tepes and picnicked with Pizarro...

New Age-Conservative-Feminist-Republicans

On The Endangered Ideology List

© 2012 James LaFond

A Note from Your Friendly Extraterrestrial Anthropologist

Recently I have come out of the closet concerning my identity [No, not that closet!]; meaning that I now freely admit to being an extraterrestrial. Never fear, I am peaceful; a mere anthropologist. My pursuit of the combat arts is simply an aspect of my immersive style of field work. If I were a clinician I would have just stayed on my home planet. My specialty is extinction events, and since it is widely theorized that human extinction events [If you don't believe in human extinction events ask the Tasmanians. Oh, I'm sorry, they're extinct!] are exclusively the direct or indirect result of human activities, it has fallen upon me to study your toxic ideologies. Toward this end I am composing an Endangered Ideology List. As the dog people at

13

Animal Planet have shown no inclination that they will permit this to be aired as a documentary, I intend to publish my notes here.

Disclaimer

I am not a theologian. I have read hundreds of religious tracts and related anthropological texts. I am not however, of a 'believing' mindset, but rather an investigative one. Religious thinkers among you have stressed to me the importance of believing what one is reading where their sacred texts are concerned. This I am barred by my nature from doing. I have read the Old Testament twice, the Koran twice, the New Testament three times, and the Psalms and Apocrypha a half dozen times. This I am told makes me a neophyte, barley having dipped my mind into the great well of beliefs that comprise the three extant faiths spawned in the tumultuous Near East. Quotes taken by me from various sacred writings and presented here, though they will be analyzed to the best of my ability, will be put under my own multicultural microscope, not necessarily the worldview shared by those who composed these tracts.

On Cultivating Useful Friendships with Earthlings

I have no more friends than the normal person. The number of acquaintances I have managed to cultivate over my life is also, I think, normal. What makes me different is the polar differences, and great variety of minds I have contact with. For instance, I am involved with three streams of facebook friends, who do not cross over. Indeed, I do not relish the idea of my various hedonistic, new age and conservative friends mixing it up. It would be too painful for all concerned. I have close friends who are woman haters, and believe females should be nothing more than property. I also have close friends who are feminists. I do not wish for the two to meet in the forum of ideas.

My studies make it useful to have a variety of friends holding diverse opinions. Therefore special friends of a unique and even contradictory nature are most desirable. For instance, I have a friend who is a black, Republican, feminist, NASCAR fan who listens to classical, country and heavy metal music, and watches sappy romances on the Hallmark Channel. Unfortunately most of my friends are rather one-dimensional. So, If you know of an Inuit investment banker who worked her way through college as an auto-magazine cover model, please introduce us.

Heads up Earthlings

It is by way of concern for my diverse friends that I post this heads up. Charles, my webmaster, has asked that I not name the religious work that these quotes come from, as he does not want to be firebombed. I will honor that request. Now, to my new-age feminist friends and conservative Republican ones; I say this to you, by way of quoting an eminent practitioner of the faith that I am quoting from, 'The enemy of my enemy is my friend.'

As different as you are, you might want to make common cause where the believers of the following lines are concerned:

The Family of Imran

'their abode shall be fire; and wretched shall be the mansion of the evil doers'

The Pen

'...man of riches...We will brand him on the nostrils.'

Daybreak

In the Name of God, the Compassionate, the Merciful

'...And against the mischief of weird women...'

Abu Lahab

In the Name of God, the Compassionate, the Merciful

'LET THE hands of ABU LAHAB perish, and let himself perish!

His wealth and his gains shall avail him not.

Burned shall he be at the fiery flame,

And his wife laden with firewood,—

On her neck a rope of palm fiber.'

Analysis

Obviously Abu Lahab was someone who made money with money, pretty much a sin anywhere in the middle-ages when this wonderful verse was composed. The preceding lines were excerpted for context, just to show that resentment of the rich and suspicion of women are not exclusively the province of modern American liberals and conservatives. Curiously enough, according to the Middle Eastern medieval mindset exemplified above, those two sentiments are not mutually incompatible.

Okay, you rich guys always knew that the world was out to make you pay for your good fortune, and you weird women know who you are. I just thought that the poor misguided feminist that might decide to cohabitate with you in your nice big house might want to know about her guilt by association. I bet that palm fiber rope was really irritating to the soft female neck. But I guess it is all relative, particularly when you are being used as fuel to roast your rich husband alive.

Look out New Age-Conservative-Feminist-Republicans. There cannot be many of you, and I doubt you can take a very big demographic hit before you make it onto the Extinct Ideology List.

Secrets of the Mayan Astronomers

A Confession of an Extraterrestrial Anthropologist

© 2012 James LaFond

Dear Pre-Apocalyptic Earthlings

The other day a blog reader told me that I made a more convincing marooned ancient astronaut than I did a human. So much for my ability to blend in! The conversation got me thinking, however, that I may, having come out of the extraterrestrial closet, have more stature as an impartial observer than I had previously suspected. This was brought home to me when that same blog reader—one of the millions you know—asked me about my theory of the Mayan prophecy, and offered a pretty good one himself.

Guilt was mine.

You people of this world fear this event in your bones, even when you joke about it. And I, sitting here with the answer have done nothing to alleviate your suffering. And dear Charles, my human assistant, the latest in a millennia-long line of human confidants to assist with my studies and polish my Orbital Egress Pod in his spacious garage, is going to be taking down the website for the coming apocalypse predicted by the ancient Mayan astronomers. Of course, he has scheduled the site to reappear like a beacon of hope in the night on 12/22/2012, the day after.

In light of these developments I thought it only right that I should unburden my soul—yes, they are not exclusive to terrestrial life forms. I have often considered doing this in an academic setting. However, my evidence in the form of my 2,300-year old field notes, are missing. I am going out on the limb here, risking the censure of my university, and even the retroactive dissolution of my research grant...

Notes on Transmigratory Fieldwork

The Native Americans understood me so well, and the Hindus get it, they really do. But the rest of you seem not to understand the inconvenient nature of transmigratory fieldwork. You see, when this particular earth body expires I must find another. I won't boor you with the details. Let's just say it is not an exact process. It's not like I can just hop demon-like into Charles and inherit the fruits of this portion of my labor, as well as his assets and family. For this reason I must make provisions, such as I did in the dawn of history, at the end of my 11th terrestrial season of fieldwork, when my aged body began to fail.

I cannot remember the exact date. If I was a mathematical prodigy I would have been permitted to stay on my home planet and reproduce! I had made a discovery that would be of much interest to future generations of Earthlings. It is easy to relocate the Orbital Egress Pod. And do not expect me to let that secret out here. I know how prone you Earthlings are to theft.

Oh, excuse my prejudice. But really, if 100% of crime on this planet is committed by Earthlings what then is an extraterrestrial observer to deduce from this?

In any case, after recording the content of this particular meeting of leading stone-age astronomers, I made three, what I intended as imperishable, recordings. I fashioned one of silver and set it up on a pedestal at my landing place, at Machu Picchu. Another was carved on the Nazca plain; the third on gold tablets which were hidden in what later became upstate New York.

So much for my skills of artifact preservation! Now I know why my application for collections management was rejected.

The Inca sent away for the silver plaque to ransom himself from Pizarro, and it was duly melted down along with his body.

The tribe I put in charge of the Nazca record were apparently aspiring comic book artists and just made a big mess out of the whole thing, completely obscuring the pictographic record that I had so diligently inscribed there, burning up most of my fuel reserves in the process.

And, some eccentric fellow with a messiah complex apparently stumbled upon my golden tablets in the early 1800s. When I confronted his successor in Salt Lake City in 1858 he threatened to have me whipped by his many wives and had his Piute friends take me to San Francisco where I was abducted—but I digress. Suffice it to say that the record of the meeting I am about to describe to you exists only in the crowded precincts of this over-worked ape's brain I am borrowing from a battered member of your species [I think it is actually damaged.] for the purpose of archiving my own work. This is like hiring a retired boxer to do your accounting.

The Conclave of Mayan Astronomers

There were four of us, three astronomers and myself, the ancient astronaut observer, kind of like the visiting scientific dignitary. They called me Feathered-Rain-Serpent.

The senior man was Puma-Star, dignified but unimaginative.

The second man was Three-Vampires-Crawling, the best mathematician; a genius really.

The junior man, just past 40, was Dog-Star, my roommate.

There we stood, around the altar in the chamber beneath the observatory. I will reconstruct the conversation as best I can, leaving out the formalities and ritual, which comprised the bulk of it.

Puma-Star: "Three-Vampires-Crawling, have you completed the sacred cyclic calculations?"

Three-Vampires-Crawling: "Yes, I have calculated the movement of the planets and the stars for the next two-thousand-three-hundred years. Do you want me to add a cycle?"

Dog-Star: "What do you want these brutes to think they are going to live forever! It is bad enough that they usurped the priesthood from us. And just today they threw the best looking girl in the region into the Sacred Well! An ugly one would have served just as well in the darkness of the underworld—let them fear the end-times."

Puma-Star: "Give it a break. Yes, a world ruled by warriors is not something that we want to seem to be sanctioning with an endless cyclic world. But think of the farmers. They cling to the land in fear as it is. Let them think that their inheritors at least will go on and on."

Three-Vampires-Crawling: "Feathered-Rain-Serpent, whether we decide to calculate a perpetual cycle or determine to stop calculating at the point that I have selected—and mind you it is an alignment, a deep one—we would appreciate your sanction. Perhaps you might endorse my calculations and my colleagues' observations. As a visitor to this world your opinion will surely carry weight down through the ages."

Feathered-Rain-Serpent: "Friends, I am honored to be present, and to have the pleasure of observing your methods. But, if my academic experience on my home planet is any guide, I must decline to endorse your work. You see if future Earthlings know that I was here, they will disparage your scientific accomplishments, as simply the copying of my knowledge. You will be depicted as no better than a monkey who imitates a man."

Dog-Star: "So they threw your girl in a well too?"

Feathered-Rain-Serpent: "Not exactly, however I was not permitted to reproduce before being sent here. This was a political action, but was really based on my low GPA."

Puma-Star: "Yes, the warlike rulers of all people have both coveted and disparaged our kind. But, none-the-less we serve them. What about the calculations? Do we have Three-Vampires-Crawling plot another cycle and then sanction it? Or do we let the rulers and the people think it will all end on some arbitrary date. And if so, do we assign observation-based meaning to this—perhaps the alignment he spoke of—or leave it to the war-priests and their cronies to interpret? Surely our kind, the thinkers among men, shall never lead again. Our day is past. So let the three of us decide how best to serve the New World Order."

The four of us paused for long moments while the legless slave-boy beat a dirge on the drum outside by the sacrificial altar. Having meditated as night covered the land, the three ancient astronomers opened their eyes, as if greeting a new day, and looked at one another; and, I am proud to say, me—the poorest theoretical mathematician in my class...

Puma-Star: "I say let us give hope. Let us place two more World Cycles on the calendar."

Dog-Star: "I say let them sweat. By the Underworld, let's just redact everything back to forty years from now, and let that brat they're grooming to take over sweat his balls off on the throne."

Three-Vampires-Crawling: "I'll do another cycle of calculations. I best head out immediately. I don't know how much longer my eyes will hold up."

So, we all clasped arms and nodded our plumed heads and followed the best mathematician in the land out onto the observatory stairs—where he tripped over the little drummer boy and fell face first, down the 80 limestone steps to his death. There I stood between Puma-Star and Dog-Star, who, as usual, managed to have the last word, "That settles it; the both of us together aren't as smart as that man. I guess the world ends where he stopped factoring—calculating—extrapolating—whatever! I need a drink."

I must admit to tying one on with Dog-Star that night. It sure beat hovering around Puma-Star as the drummer boy was tortured and executed.

The God of Things

The Native American End-time Prediction that
Came True

© 2013 James LaFond

Author's Note
Since writing this piece I have read more
than 20 additional books on the subject. I would
like to add, that on no other continent conquered by
Anglo-Europeans has such reverence for native
place names [particularly of rivers] been equaled.
The warriors that died fighting many of the longest
rearguard actions in military history, and the holy
men that advised them, literally still haunt this land,
from the names of the rivers we canoe on, to the
name for that ingenious little boat, to the tactics of
our modern special warfare soldiers, and most of all
in the person of the rural deer hunter so much
despised by our current political establishment.
There seemed to have been a sense all along, that
there was something to be learned from the
American Indian, even as an enemy.

-5/13/2014

"The greatest object of their lives seems to be to acquire possessions—to be rich. They desire to possess the whole world...their Great Chief compels every man to pay him for the land he lives upon and all his personal goods—even those he needs for his own existence—every year. I am sure we could not live under such a law."

-Ohiyesa's uncle

From Your Friendly Extraterrestrial Anthropologist

"I will ask him to help me understand his ways, then I will prepare the way for my children. Maybe they will outrun the white man in his own shoes."

-Many Horses

We have recently discussed the Mayan prophecy of our worldwide doom on this site. I have given a few weeks time before emerging from my ancient astronaut version of a white-supremacist bunker to declare the danger past; even illusory. There are others waiting in the wings of our dread too; the Hopis in the Southwest have an end-time prediction I am told, and one must remember that not all ancient astronauts are as benign as I am.

31

That is because they are not from Regal, my superior system, but from Sirius—those people are worse than the Alpha Centurions and should be—but I digress. Back to your more pressing terrestrial squabbles...

Recently a reader asked me if I believed in prophecies and predictions and if I thought there had been any sustainable predictions made by Native Americans. What follows is my answer, which necessitates some setup.

My working theory is as follows: that, after hundreds of years of direct and indirect contact with European invaders, Native American visionaries and war-leaders decided A. that the white menace could not be resisted and that their way of life was doomed; and B. that the white way of life was tantamount to a spiritual death sentence upon all of humanity, and it was therefore desirable to perish defiantly instead of join the white man in his evil pursuits.

There were many variations on this, and many Native Americans who physically survived did so at the cost of their values. While the war-chiefs perished the last visionaries did make an attempt to project into the white man's future a vision of what they saw as the truth; a world of spirit rather than a world of things. I suspect, as these folks did not generally expect their blood lines to survive, that these messages were given to the whites that recorded their words in hopes that some white man in the distant future might come to his senses and see the world as it had, or might have, been.

For further reading see Cleanse the Land and Someone Has Got Our Horses on this site.

My Perspective and Bias

"How smooth must be the language of the whites, when they can make right look like wrong, and wrong look like right."

-Black Hawk

I have two friends with some Native American blood who will refuse to read this—because I don't, as a white have the right to comment on the subject of Native Americans.

Likewise, those that know me understand my penchant for the underdog and can expect me to be biased in the favor of the losers in any conflict. As far as my own ancestry I was told by my French

Canadian grandmother that she had one uncle killed by Indians around the great lakes and that her father, Elzear, had an Indian friend by the name of 'Mister Short-step.' It seems to be a hereditary bias wash there.

I will attempt to be unbiased. However, since I largely reject the mores of our current society, my claim to unbiased coverage should be held as suspect, and the following my opinion, except where I can offer checkable arguments, like in the military section below. I must admit though, that I watched a lot of westerns as a kid in which I cheered on the Indian-killing heroes. If my Cherokee friend got this far he's probably clicking off the site as you read this line.

The Martial Overview

"In war they have leaders and war-chiefs of different grades. The common warriors are driven forward like a herd of antelope to face the foe. It is because of this manner of fighting—from compulsion and not from personal bravery—that we count no coup [take no credit] on [for killing] them. A lone warrior can do much harm to a large army of them—especially when they are in unfamiliar territory."

-Ohiyesa's uncle

When I suggest that the Native American warrior of North America was generally superior and outfought his European counterpart, my military history buff friends [all white guys] howl with indignation. Yes we did, after 400 years of setbacks, win. The Mongol khans would laugh—they conquered more people and more land in 40 years than the British, American, French, Canadian, Spanish and Mexican military establishments did in aggregate over 400 years.

Many of my friends still hold to the belief that the white is a genetically superior killer and has hence conquered the globe. I have some black friends who believe this too; that whites are like poorly treated pit-bulls, prone to killing. The question is not one of genetics but of culture. In Central and South America a few thousand Spanish conquistadors wiped out and conquered millions in a few decades. In North America a few thousand Native warriors withstood and terrorized millions for hundreds of years.

This is the dynamic of hunter versus city-slicker. The conquistadors hunted down and exterminated the urbanized Aztecs, Mayans and Incas, with methods perfected against the Moors and Canary Islanders over hundreds of years. The interesting fact is that the Indians never saw it as a genetic question. To them the white man was an inferior warrior only because of how he lived. This contention was borne out to their sorrow when the best and most effective warriors on the frontier turned out to be white men who had lived like the Native warrior: Lewis Millet; Simon Girty; Simon Kenton; Blue Jacket; Kit Carson...

Eventually the adoption of their own ways by a small cadre of enemies permitted those dauntless men to lead the ever multiplying hordes of non-warrior soldiers into the interior, from where they could resist the Natives from within fortified positions. The writing was really on the wall when the Union military, after losing virtually every battle to the Confederate military during the Civil War, won the war through attrition.

When an industrialized nation finds the will to kill, it can only be stopped by a bigger economic engine that out-produces it; as the Nazi war machine was ground to dust while inflicting 15 to 1 casualties against the Soviets and 3 to 1 casualties against the Allies in World War Two.

It has ever been the curse on warrior societies that their attention to virtue over gain produces less weaponry, fewer weapon-wielders, and less supply to sustain hostilities. As technology progresses and casualties mount this, not excellence, becomes the key to victory; with the mediocre mass prevailing over the elite few. During the same period that the Indian was driven to extinction and the Confederate warrior was starved into a barefoot skeletal killer, the Japanese were giving up warrior ethics for industrial mores at the same time; resulting, by the 1930s, in the singularly most horrific killing machine ever let loose on the field of battle [check into the Rape of Nanking]; fortunately devoured by the might of American industry.

Virtually the entire history of warfare can be viewed as elite predation on the effeminate masses, followed by mediocre aggression-by-attrition upon the society that supports the elite warriors that once ruled the battlefield. Napoleon should not have been surprised when Britain—that damned 'nation of shopkeepers'—would prevail over his warrior nation.

To their credit the Native American war-chiefs and peace-chiefs generally saw this coming a long way off and were not blindsided by the defeat of their warriors at the hands of inferior slave-soldiers.

The Spiritual Context

"We send our little Indian boys and girls to school, and when they come back talking English, they come back swearing. There is no swear word in the Indian languages, and I haven't yet learned to swear."

-Zitkala-Sa

As a writer I am uncomfortable discussing religion and spirituality in a nonfiction format. To me spirituality and its state of social bondage [religion] are deeply subjective and are most appropriately explored through fiction. If you want to examine some variances and enjoy divergent spiritual and religious viewpoints than I suggest any of my Sunset Saga novels featuring Three-Rivers, Randy Bracken or Richard F. Burton.

This is not a primer on Native American beliefs. I just want you to be suspicious in your own readings of the fact that most of their stated beliefs came to us through Christian translators and transcribers [sometimes negatively, and sometimes positively, biased]. When they could put their own theological pen to paper, they had already been living under Christian influence for generations.

My personal impression, my vision of how the Native American spiritualists saw Christianity, is based on the writings of Red Jacket, Ohiyesa, Black Elk, and Chief Seattle, and has a Tolkienesque spin.

To me the vision of the last Native spiritualists was one of the Christian God as a dark lord; presiding over a bleak gutted land of things. To nature worshipping traditionalists a God that sanctions ecological warfare can be nothing but evil. I know I am treading on thin ice here, equating the Biblical Almighty with the ethereal villain of a blood-drenched fairytale. But honestly, I think Tolkien did a better job of painting the picture that was the Native American window on the world of the late 19th Century, in his epic work, than I could here.

If you are old enough to remember the 1991 Gulf War, then you probably shared my horror when the Iraqi dictator set fire to the Kuwaiti oil fields to cover his army's retreat. That act elicited a worldwide gasp of horror. Imagine, if our entire world ecology was attacked like that? That is what the Native Americans witnessed, an attack upon their planet—not just them—by an alien invader; a successful attack.

The Package Deal Protestant Sermon

"It is recorded of him [Jesus Christ] that a bruised reed he never broke. Cease, then, to call yourselves Christians, lest you declare to the world your hypocrisy. Cease, too, to call other nations savage, when you are tenfold more the children of cruelty then they."

-Thayendanegea

We now see Christianity, as it is marketed in a heavily materialistic postindustrial world, as a value system devoid, even opposed to, materialism. You must understand, however, that the material products, weaponry, and even whiskey produced by European and later American industry, was presented by white evangelicals, as well as military and civic leaders packing The Bible for their own purposes, as one in the same. The entire European economic system, including chattel slavery, was depicted as a result—indeed the promised benefits of—adherence to the Scripture and Gospels that comprised The Bible.

So, when a Native American was 'witnessed to' in the 19th Century and before, he was being sold an entire lifeway; everything from the suit and the haircut to the eradication of the Buffalo and the superiority of whites over red-men, black-men and yellow-men, as part and parcel of the Christian experience.

The 18th and 19th Century Native American rejection of Christian/industrialism has its closest parallel in the American rejection of Nazi Germany and the Ku Klux Klan in the second half of the 20th Century.

Note: In the 1920s and 30s Nazism and the KKK were—to a shocking degree by our modern standards—accepted as forces for moral good by white America.

My sister belongs to a young non-denominational Christian congregation. My mother attends Catholic mass. When I attend services with these ladies I listen to sermons that would have closer parallels with Native American ethics lectures in the mid 1800s then what was then being preached from

Christian pulpits. If you brought a good Christian preacher foreword in a time-machine from 1850s America he would either end up selling sealant on late night infomercials or preaching ethnic cleansing on a neo-Nazi website.

Just as the modern idea of what constitutes political liberalism has reversed poles from the 1800s to present, so has the idea of what it is to be Christian. I tuned into the Christian Broadcast Network recently, and heard not a word in favor of military conquest, racial superiority, or ecological exploitation.

The Elements of Native Rejection

"We do not want churches because they will teach us to quarrel about God, as the Catholics and Protestants do. We do not want to learn that."

-Chief Joseph

The major points of the rejection of Christian/Industrial values by Native Americans in North America are as follows:

1. White children are treated badly, and when adopted after capture into Indian families never wish to return to their white parents.

2. A white husband and wife are regarded as owner and property whereas an Indian husband and wife are regarded as partners.

3. Men who come of age in white society cannot fight and therefore will not be able to protect their society from evil.

4. White elders are discarded and set aside rather than being cherished and consulted for their wisdom.

5. The equating of the teachings of Jesus to the tenets of European warfare and capitalist industry are so ludicrous that any preacher or leader extolling the two as compatible –let alone as a seamless life ethic—can be regarded as nothing other than deluded or hypocritical.

Voices of the End-time

"Death will come, always out of season."

-Big Elk

Ohiyesa, who was actually educated at a major university and was instrumental in the formation of the Boy Scouts of America, stated that white society or 'civilization' was 'a way of living based on trade'. He admitted that it was good for the accumulation of goods, the expansion of population and the subjugation of traditional [primitive] peoples. He did his best, without risking the leveling of intolerable insults at the conquering society who had tolerated him as a convert, to offer warnings: that religion-as-mind-control; rampant materialism; and ecological subjugation as an economic model were not sustainable in the long term.

Part of the three conclusions above is based on my reading between his lines. He was treading on thin ice, attempting to preach ethics and ecology to a nation that was embracing the KKK in the White House and hanging black men for sport every day. If he had any hope that his words would survive to be read during some distant awakening of conscience among the descendents of those who had conquered his people, and raped his home, then he had to talk softly; in a whisper that would hopefully travel across the generations to be heard by someone morally equipped to listen.

Since you now insist on eating tuna that has not resulted in the tormented death of your closest aquatic relative, perhaps you are so equipped.

The Native View of Industrial/Christian Supremacy

"If my warriors are to fight they are too few; if they are to die they are too many."

-Hendrick

Once the hope of a society has been lost, the leaders tend to focus on trying to preserve a trace of their people. For some, like Many Horses, it comes down to an attempt to prepare his descendents to survive a long cultural night, in hopes that there will be a morning somewhere down through the ages; like a hope for a second coming, a chance for a rebirth.

For others, like Ohiyesa, it comes down to an attempt to craft a message that might be heard by some future generation of his conqueror's offspring, to preserve a voice for his people.

Chief Seattle, was, I think, one of the later, an admonishing ghost, serving up a reminder for those who drove his kind to extinction, though he uses the terms 'dust' and 'mist'.

Resonant Warning or Bleak Affirmation

"It is but an old woman's dream. Then I see but shadows and hear only the roar of the river, and tears come into my eyes. Our Indian life, I know, is gone forever."

-Waheenee

What is the Native American End-time prophecy that I suggested in the title?

A world where the young are neglected and abused…

A world that has been raped and stripped of its natural resources...

A world where some Great Chief is supported by involuntary gifts demanded from the common man, actually living in a 'great house' at public expense...

A world of hypocrisy, whose leaders and holy men do not abide by the laws and ethics they extol…

Take Me To Your Breeder

A world in which people care so much about material possessions that they, themselves, become nothing but the material possessions of others...

A world where the virtues of a warrior are nothing before the devil's workshop of death-dealing devices controlled by the Great Chief...

A world where the old are cast aside, separated from the young ones they should be educating and the adults they should be advising; having returned to the status of their childhood; either abused or neglected just as they began their lives among us.

This is the collective prediction of the long-dead Native American spiritualists, a number of warnings based on long observation of those who hunted them across the face of what had once been their world.

I hope none of the above predictions come to pass.

I would not get too worried, however, unless four out of the seven dire predictions actually come to pass.

-Extraterrestrially yours, Regal M-116-S

Interview with an Extraterrestrial Anthropologist

On Foreign Affairs and American Residency

© 2013 Regal M-116-S

The following is the reprint of a blog piece I did this past fall in 2012. Being aggressively interviewed by a teenager was an unexpected exprience that I rushed right home and documented. It was this conversation that first convinced me that it was time I admitted to my alien nature.

The Innerpost of Empire

Today I was approached by a teenager who sees himself as being at odds with the world. He knows me to be a writer and decided to pick my brain about a wide variety of issues. At the end of our conversation, after he had declared me to be surprisingly moderate on religion and culture, and frighteningly obtuse musically, he finally turned to what concerns his father, international affairs. I prefaced this final stage of our conversation with, "You are about to understand why my family and friends are uncomfortable with my worldview, which might ultimately be the reason I write."

"So, what do you think we should do in Iraq?"

"We? I am not in Iraq. We are not in Iraq thank God."

"As a Citizen of the United States do you think we should pull out of Iraq by Twenty-fourteen?"

"I regard the affairs of Iraq as none of my business."

"You mean you do not consider yourself a citizen of this country?"

"I was born on the portion of this continent ruled by the U.S. By birth I am a slave to this nation. The government taxes me and does what it will with the take. I am an 'owned' asset of the U.S. It is against the law for me to end my own life. I can abide by its laws, or I can abide by the laws of some other, even more intrusive, nation, or I can abide by the laws of some penal institution. I choose the path of least resistance, and so abide by the laws of this nation and municipalities therein."

"That is astounding. I no longer think of myself as a radical. You view life like an inmate and you're okay with that?"

"I do not imagine myself fighting a revolution, or thinking I could change things through politics. I can't get my sister to see things my way. What sense would it be for me to expect the rest of the people in this country to agree with me?"

"So you don't think we should use the government to make things better?"

"I consider it immoral to impose my will on another person outside of a sporting or imminent survival context. Most people are fearful, greedy and stupid. Therefore fear, greed and stupidity are the cornerstones of political life. Why do I want to get all mixed up in that process as a vested protagonist?"

"Okay, as a human being what do you think about the current U.S. military presence in Iraq and Afghanistan?"

"I am glad the most powerful military machine in human history is elsewhere."

"Okay then"—laughter—"as a student of history what do you think of current U.S. military involvement overseas?"

"I am really interested how the Afghan situation will pan out. Will the U.S. do any better than the Soviets, or the Brits? Now Iraq is the excretion cleft of the Middle East, so I don't expect long term peace there. From the U.S. perspective Afghanistan makes sense if you control the heroin production and distribution, and then use military force to open third world nations for importation of the product."

"That is disgusting. What kind of sick country would do that?"

"The Brits did, and the U.S. helped them, in the nineteen-hundreds."

"Okay, I think I can guess this one. What do you think of the police, of their arrogant demeanor, their nice white cars, their guns, the fact that they think they are better than you and me?"

"I think it is justified. Every police officer is, by the standards of society at large, better than I am. They make more money than me. They are permitted to impose their will on others in the name of the rest of us, and they have nice white cars and guns."

"Really, doesn't it bother you that they are so arrogant, that they jack us up for just walking down this street?"

"No. They should be arrogant. Their job is to impose social will. That requires a skill set that begs for arrogance as a personality trait, and the job description will most likely cultivate it in those where it is not preexisting. They are, after all, 'my master's loyal slaves', the men with the whips in their hands! I would be deluded to expect them to treat me as an equal. I'm the outsider on the inside."

"You write sci-fi. So what about space travel or intergalactic intelligence?"

"We are a bunch of chimps bashing each other's heads in with coconuts on an island. If any aliens have discovered us they've sped by us like New Yorkers making sure not to stop in Camden."

"Do you consider yourself to be highly intelligent?"

"I hope I am not among the brightest. If I am, then we're going to be stuck here on Chimp Island forever, hitting each other with coconuts."

"How about if I put my coconut on the end of a stick?"

"Now you're getting it kid."

War Heroes of Planet Obadrone

The Return of Your Friendly Neighborhood
Extraterrestrial Anthropologist

© 2013 James LaFond

Charles has been unable to remove the centuries of corrosion from my orbital egress pod, so it seems I'm stuck—in a fast wearing out little ape's body at that! Ever since I failed my Galactic Civil Service exam, and was sterilized and launched down the spiral arm of the galaxy that you earthlings have so hideously misnamed after a dairy-based confection, to work out my 10,000 year sentence on this stingy Extinction Event Grant, I have entertained myself at the ends of my various terrestrial lives by observing your dreadful propensity for mutual extermination contests.

Why, if it would not be an intergalactic war crime, I would suggest to the High Council at Regal that about a million of you violent little felons be packed into the largest asteroid in the system and launched at Andromeda! I think it is a smashing idea really, no doubt influenced by my many thousands of years' education at your collective blood-soaked knee. However, as much as I despise the Andromedeans I would not risk being drummed out of the Galactic Zoological Association after your inevitable war crimes were brought to light. Really, one more misstep and I'll be recording solar flare temperatures from Mercury.

In fact—and I do not mean to crush your little egos—your existence is even being questioned by my superiors. Little apes running around stabbing each other with inventively fabricated implements for eons they believed. But when I sent my last report on that World War Two event, some rivals who have long been jealous of my vacation like exile on this quaint little planet, accused me of writing fiction! I'm almost afraid to send my latest report concerning your flying robots. In fact I've chickened out already, and am instead circulating it among you, making another call for unlikely mutual simian sanity through this hairy little malfunctioning LaFond organism I've been stuck in for the past fifty years—good Galaxy the last three digits of the right claw do not even extend all the way to the keyboard! I'm going to demand a refund on this one...

Since this sack of bones is becoming increasingly difficult to navigate in, and Charles is still refusing to purchase me one of those automobiles—it's old technology really—I was recently scouring online newspapers for news of some heroic bloodbath in the Hindu Kush. Your wars used to be so brutally fun to read about. You savage little primates have always been so dramatically colorful about the whole business. I really do miss all of your sharp shiny sticks!

One of my favorites happened in the Kyber Pass, when thousands of overdressed British soldiers, their poorly educated officers, and all of their expensive baggage and lady friends, were ambushed and slaughtered by fanatical Afghan tribesmen. Well, the fanatical Afghan tribesmen are still there. But instead of haughty British officers trying to appear more brave than the Light Brigade charging the Russian guns at in the Crimea with 'jolly good cheer' we've got your next door neighbor's brat kid playing video games at a computer console in D.C. while some DOD suit struts around behind him pumping his fist, "Yeah

Fuckmed, Uncle Slam is recalling that Toyota four-by-four in nine, eight, seven...”

Wow, even war is lame these days. Perhaps you primates might consider planetary science?

Welcome to Planet Obadrone

2012 U.S. payroll for mercenary soldiers and the assorted teamsters, pilots, construction workers and landscapers [and their considerable material] required to move and house them [I'm sorry but I was unable to determine if their meals were included. So, if I have left any commissary clerks or cooks out of the budget, I apologize.]: that would be 516 billion of your devalued dollars

-source, Nile Bowie, a little commie squeak hiding out in Malaysia, who has for some reason of late been demonstrating a pathological fear of model planes

Civilian casualties claimed by various Pakistani sources from U.S. Obadrone strikes: 1,990-3,308, depending on how many fingers the Islamic journalist in question had remaining to use his abacus. The Pakistani militants are claiming that 50 civilians are killed by Obadrone strike to every 1 alleged terrorist blown to shreds.

57

-source, biased, Islamic and positively medieval

The portion of the above Obadrone strike kills confirmed by a U.S. intelligence source: 482 killed, 265 of which were known to not be members of the terrorist group that destroyed your twin towers, and 6 of whom were known to be leaders of that same unsavory group.

-source, anonymous U.S. intelligence source, who is even now being interviewed in Dick Chaney's basement by a Bosnian corrections contractor with a blow-torch

The number of Pakistani 'Good Samaritans' who were targeted and killed by follow up Obadrone strikes while rendering first aid to, or scraping up the remains of, the original Obadrone assassination target: 50

-source, some loud mouthed traitor named Ben Emerson

The number of innocent bystanders killed by Obadrone strikes targeting the funeral processions of already dead targets [My, what thorough little beasties you are!]: 20

-source, the same commie bastard as above

Percentage of Obadrone kills that are [excuse me, were] targeted individuals: 2% [Indicating that 98% of those killed have thoughtlessly caused plummeting housing values for their distraught surviving neighbors.]

-source, the 'socialist' University of the 'People's Republic' of New York State

The name of the video game medal being awarded to UAV Drivers [kids sitting in Washington D.C. operating a joystick to kill distant barefoot enemies]: Distinguished Warfare Medal

-source, Associated Press

The number of Pakistani [I did not know you American primates were at war with your Pakistani counterparts.] civilians killed in the first 10 days of 2013: 11 [Not impressive really. West Baltimore teenagers killed as many unarmed Civilians with handguns in the same period.]

-source, Roosky Television

The response by United States Senator and humanitarian Lindsey Graham, when questioned about 'extrajudicial killings' by Obadrones, "We've killed four thousand seven hundred...sometimes you [I guess he is speaking to the video game kid.] hit innocent people, and I hate that, but we are at war..."

-source, RT.com [I like that Putin hires all of his female newscasters from New York strip clubs.]

Enjoy your heroic war my terrestrial fiends—I mean friends. Charles, is the bunker insolated yet? What about air conditioning? Are you sure? Yes thank you...have you located any suitable females who might be receptive to me in my current state of deterioration? Charles? Charles!

-Regal M-116-S

The Viking Hammerlock

Dark Age Dating Lore from Your Extraterrestrial Wingman

© 2013 James LaFond

As an extraterrestrial anthropologist I have spent many a lifetime as one of you—always a man I might add, never wanting to be a member of that off-prodded gender we so adore. Recently, over drinks with a lady friend, I was stricken with deja vu. While the Viking Hammerlock is not combat, it is a functional adjunct to a warrior's second favorite pastime. Also, in the interest of good taste, and knowing that our lady readers do not read from the Ancient Combat Page, I have hidden this bit of advice for dealing with the distaff gender in plain sight as it were.

Raggar the Leg-splitter

Whilst residing in Iceland some 1,000 years past consulting on the recording of those people's Sagas, I made the acquaintance of this chieftain who did most of his reaving behind closed doors. One of the perks of transmigratory fieldwork among human kind is my ability to tap into the lessons of lives lost, of course, only when my mind is jogged by a deep racial memory.

The drinks I was recently sharing with a female friend then brought to mind a woman, who brought to mind Raggar and his hammerlock, thus resulting in this paper, which I intend to submit to the Nobel Committee next year.

Mrs. Bedwrecker

Nearly a decade past, not long after being fired by yet another mate, I found myself crashing in Ajay's girl cave. This alternatively living lady permitted me to set up my gladiatorial barracks in the back room of her condo, where I did occasionally entertain visiting female dignitaries.

My favorite was a certain Mrs. Bedwrecker. This lady usually brought along a hot cappuccino, often arriving in nothing but a heavy coat and high heels. She also provided me with alcoholic beverages and large plastic ware encased meals—which Raggar would have been most jealous of. The thing that most commended Mrs. Bedwrecker to the unattached ETA was the fact that she was the property of another man, and therefore became his concern where all of the least pleasurable things in life were concerned. I was therefore not required to lay aside my sword for the odious business of haggling over furniture, or to demean my sword arm arranging the drapery, or to engage in that most pointless pursuit of slaying grass at her behest.

There was, however, a problem with my gladiatorial accommodations. You see, my single piece of furniture consisted of a mattress, and the lady liked to sit and sip her molten cappuccino as she plied me with liquor and insist I dazzle her with the contents of my millennial mind. We settled the cappuccino issue by agreeing that she might seat herself across my hips and gaze down upon me while we conversed.

I was, however stymied, when trying to arrange for my own drinks without unseating Mrs. Bedwrecker who very much preferred to keep her seat and wished with equal sincerity to render me helpless through drink. I, at first, resisted these attempts on my sobriety, afraid that I might be compromised Samson-like and placed under the power of my enemies. However, I reminded myself that I, in this wretched life, occupy no position of importance, find myself woefully lacking in noteworthy enemies, and was only in danger of being delivered up to the attentions of this very agreeable lady.

'What to do?' I thought.

Then I recalled Raggar's technique for the ergonomic use of serving wenches from a prone position!

Here it is my fellow warriors. And even if you be a Neanderthal gnawing on the haunch of meat proffered by your seated lady, or some civilized sot being fed grapes by your slave girl, or a hordesman enjoying fermented mare's milk from the scented hand of your latest booty, this technique should prevent you from choking Attila-like on your particular beverage of relish, without unseating your dutiful servant.

Sit up.

Bend your shield arm behind your lower back as a brace.

Reach out with your sword arm to take over management of your beverage so that your wench might busy herself with more pressing concerns.

Lean back upon the brace of your shield arm, and enjoy a draught or three while you enjoy the show.

Feminist Addendum

If, my friend, you find yourself mounted by one of these willful verbal amazons that go by the disconcerting name of 'feminist', heed me. Mrs. Bedwrecker was a member of this female tribe of disputatious scholars. I bid you learn from my misfortune and not your own. If, when employing the Viking hammerlock in pursuit of such agreeably seated company, you find yourself recalling that Raggar's women were known as wenches, do not make the mistake of referring to your Amazonian mistress by way of this sobriquet, particularly if her cappuccino is still piping hot—as such drinking engagements are typically pursued shirtless.

You have been warned.

Take Me To Your Breeder

Extraterrestrially yours, Regal M-116-S

Pops Takes One For The Team

Your Extraterrestrial Anthropologist on the Slaughter of Your Elders

© 2014 James LaFond

On New Year's Eve I was observing your cyclic chronologic rites from the comfort of a suburban retreat alongside of some of your more elderly co-inhabitants. I have often dreaded these times because of these elderly earthlings' acceptance of the baseless pronouncements made by their media handlers. Then again, I owe you're TV ranch hands for corralling their minds with petty concerns. For this was the very means of my most recent awakening. When I noticed that my human caretakers believed all of this drivel, and also knowing them not to be stupid or insane, I came to the conclusion that they were subject to mind-control through the TV oracle around which their domestic gathering place was structured.

You see, when this aging host expires, and I transmigrate into the body of some ill-fated fetus—hopefully not in Juarez of Mogadishu—and am thereby placed in the horrifyingly inept care of some stupid earthlings, it will take some time before I realize that I am not one of you. Then I will have to go about the odious process of relocating my orbital pod, convincing Charles that I am the actual reincarnation of Regal M-116-S, in the process overcoming his sentimental attachment to this LaFond avatar, and then somehow, well, you know the drill by now. Fieldwork is simply not what it used to be back when I partied with Mayan astronomers.

So, I sat through the story of the Maryland State Fireworks Prohibitions being defeated in the most farcical manner. It is illegal to own or use fireworks in Maryland and Pennsylvania. It is, in Maryland, likewise illegal to traffic in fireworks. In Pennsylvania, however, it is legal to buy fireworks if, you are not a Pennsylvanian, and you sign a form promising to remove these noxious world-ending death-ray devices to another state—that being Maryland, which happens to be a stone-throw from the retail outlets in question!

Next was a note about cleansing foods, to purge your nasty digestive tracts of the toxins you presumably shoveled into them in massive quantities over the past month.

There was then news of football bowl games. Vlad would have been pleased—excepting the excessive contact rulings that have recently been impinging on the dignity of this war game.

Then things heated up with a still photograph of three vicious looking white men in hip hop Jessie James outfits robbing a bank. I was beginning to develop interest in your predatory habits again, when news that another one of your elderly World War Two veterans was beaten and robbed by young thugs. The 89-year-old man, a member of your 'greatest generation', was out walking between 6 and 7 a.m. Three teenagers in dark clothing attacked him, struck him on the head with something, and then robbed him of his cash.

Little information about the victim was reported, in contrast to a recent attack on an 89-year-old black man in Texas.

The media shepherd then announced that nothing else was known of the attackers, which was an obvious lie, as the victim had been able to identify the color of their clothing. She then pleaded for help in identifying these thugs who she was protecting by failing to identify their known racial characteristics.

Now, based on the photo of those three white bank robbers, and the fact that that crime took place in the same suburban municipality as the mugging of your collective lingering hero, I was naturally curious as to whether or not these thugs were white, black, or Hispanic, particularly since gang activity by all three ethnic groups is on the rise in that county.

Why has the race of these attackers been withheld, when it was declared across the country a mere two weeks ago that a beastly white man beat a black elder?

I do know that two white WWII veterans have been killed by teenage black attackers in the U.S. in 2013.

Also, last week, there were calls in New York for stiffer penalties against black teens who attack Jewish men in the 'knockout game', with one lawmaker stipulating that attacks that are not part of a robbery should be prosecuted as hate crimes.

This notion that our elder in the town of Millersville is less a victim of violence because he was robbed, as opposed to some investment banking analyst being sucker-punched for juvenile enjoyment, strikes me as obscene. Then again, I'm not one of you quirky little apes, but a toiling anthropologist working off a research grant with some pretty draconian stipulations attached to it.

It also strikes me as obscene that the known racial identity of the man's attackers is being withheld. This means one thing: that the State Media considers it more important to protect criminals from victims, than to protect victims from criminals. Indeed, if the 'news' report had stated that these boys were white, taken together with the fact that three whites just robbed that bank down the road, one might conclude that white gang activity is spiking, and that you might wish to avoid groups of white youths and young men.

If this crime had taken place in Baltimore City, where virtually all violent crime is committed by black males, it would be reasonable to assume that the attackers were black. I am guessing that these Millersville attackers were black, only based on the fact that a black law officer was interviewed about the crime, which he declared would not be tolerated. The interview had obvious propaganda overtones, although I felt an immediate kinship with the black redneck cop, surely a holdover from some bygone era.

This entire trend, the demonization of white criminals, and the obscuring of the racial makeup of non-white criminals, [believe me, when the cops talk to each other about suspects, what color they are is item number one on the conversation platform] points to State management of your violence trends. Since whites are the majority, and would reasonably constitute the main force of any domestic American insurgency, the State is letting you monkeys know in advance, that whites who defy it will suffer especially severe treatment.

The State does not fear minority groups, because, by cultivating them as a menace and keeping them at large, they gain a certain measure of leverage with the primarily passive population of whites they are charged with 'protecting'. And, should any non-white insurgency ever develop traction in this Police State, they will be easily crushed, few and localized as they are.

Furthermore, the cultivation of a violent ethnically divergent underclass by the State—as evidenced by its every policy—has naturally developed a counter-current militant ethic among demonized white males. This will insure, that in case of a social breakdown of some sort, that State forces, if they ever find themselves overtaxed, will be able to pull back and watch the three rival ethnic blocks they have created, tear each other apart. The managers of the United States Autarchy should be commended for their farseeing counterinsurgency provisions.

I feel much sympathy for the old man in Millersville who was beaten and robbed by three race-withheld attackers. He has, however sacrificed for higher ends: minority youth inclined towards violence have been emboldened to level up their reign of terror and continue exporting it from urban to suburban environments; reactionary elements among the majority have been further embittered, and more likely to expose their treasonous tendencies prematurely, so that they might be dealt with ahead of whatever crises the State fears; and the poor elderly creatures that sat next to me viewing this injustice, were further terrified, indeed began discussing self-imposed curfews and later discussed their willingness to support a crime-fighting politician.

Take Me To Your Breeder

The chances of You People ever getting off of this rock in infestation-sustaining numbers continue to diminish. I am, however, impressed with earth as a potential galactic penal colony.

Extraterrestrially yours, Regal M-116-S

Anachronistically Confused

An Extraterrestrial Anthropologist Beseeches The 300-plus Geeks Who Read Anachronistically Yours

© 2014 James LaFond

A number of readers—one being Erique, a training partner [who has discovered that I'm still not used to these awkward bilateral appendages and continue to sprain my flexor tendons and ankles in sparring] who works in the comic book industry—give or loan me material to review for the site. Two people have even sent me books to review that they did not have time to read; using me as a living cliff note I suppose—talk about feeling used!

I typically begin my writing week on Monday with seven articles outlined and saved in miniature at the bottom of the screen. I also carry about 300 outlines in the various folders. Daily I check the backend of the site for comments and views, responding to the comments, and noting how the reader views are trending. For instance, if I have

200 reads today, and 150 of them are book review reads, and I have two Harm City and two book reviews outlined, I will get the reviews out there first.

Now, occasionally a piece will take off, like when MMA Gloves and Boxing got 1,000 reads in two days. Obviously some coven of cerebral knuckleheads found this article—which Fight Magazine scoffed at in 2010—to be useful. Then Charles found out it had been reposted on some site or another. That makes sense, and is flattering. As a writer it is always a weird feeling when something written years ago becomes popular. For one thing, I regard everything I wrote before 2011 as being pretty poorly crafted. I can't even bare to read stuff I wrote before 2000.

In late 2012 I wrote a piece titled Anachronistically Yours: Crawling Into the Multimedia World. It received about 50 reads over a year on the site. Of the 750 or so articles and stories posted on this site I would have to rate it at about 600, far worse than the last thing I would put in my ghost writer's application submission if I found myself attempting to whore for We Pay You To Write Big Guy.slum. The article was basically a plea to the reader, to please explain to me why I am apparently retarded when it comes to comprehending comic books.

Anachronistically Yours is now the third most read piece on this site. It has picked up over 250 reads in the past week. Still, no reader comments, "Hey, LaFond, it's because you've been punched in the head 10,000 times!"

What has happened to that crappy piece of griping, 'I'm too old to appreciate what you young bucks are into' keyboardmanship?

Are a bunch of comic geeks sitting around drinking bright blue Mountain Dew into the wee hours, taking turns reading it in imitation of me, and then applauding the geek who sounds the most like Burgess Meredith griping to Sly Stallone?

Has some Japanese biotech firm identified in me a master strain of dyslexia, their Takonori Gomi-looking white-suited Yakusa goons already on their way to Baltimore to abduct me for an excruciatingly lethal round of testing, in their quest to develop a manga speed-reading drug?

Have my fellows from school, back on Regal-S, finally noted my achievements as an extraterrestrial anthropologist? Does old M-12 stand before the Remote Viewing Portal even now, with his indicating appendage pointed at Anachronistically Yours, and his verbal orifice announcing, "There, would be students of the life way of lesser forms, there is a stroke of genius! Consider M-116's example and imbed yourself as the idiot of the population!"

Really, an expiring mind wants to know, why did you repost or link to Anachronistically Yours?

Please, let me now before this deteriorating LaFond avatar completely wears out.

Extraterrestrially Yours, Regal M-116-S

Was Slavery Truly Necessary?

The Crackpot Dropout Author is put to the Question by a Schoolteacher

© 2014 James LaFond

This morning I received an e-mail from a reader, Leah, a schoolteacher. I find it interesting how you young people attach your pictures to your e-mail account. And, can unequivocally state, that if my school teachers had looked like this chick, I would not have dropped out—hell, I'd probably still be in school.

"So, a question to you as a learned historian: was slavery truly a necessary economic step in the development of nations? And more specifically, would the US be able to develop and catch up to its European rivals without that giant free labor force working the plantations? Feel free to reference an existing work of yours or someone else that addresses the issue."

First, let me focus that question a bit more…

"So, a question to you as a **_LEARNED HISTORIAN, and extraterrestrial anthropological authority_**: was slavery truly a necessary economic step in the development of nations? And more specifically, would the US be able to develop and catch up to its European rivals without that giant free labor force working the plantations? Feel free to reference an existing work of yours or someone else that addresses the issue."

Now, that is better.

Was Slavery a Necessary Nation-building Step?

Our reader is referring to chattel slavery, which is the large scale use of humans as working livestock. This practice was at its greatest extent in the ancient world between 300 B.C. and A.D. 250. All I have to do to prove it was not necessary is to point to a functional, self sufficient nation [an amalgamation of tribes ruled by law] that was not dependent on chattel slavery. I need go no farther than the Iroquois Nation, a military power respected by American colonists for 200 years. Indeed, it is unlikely New England could have been settled by the whites without the aid of the Iroquois in wiping out the rival Algonquin tribes. Like many aborigine people of North America they did practice limited household slavery, sometimes ending in adoption. The 'longhouse people' were not, however, saints. I have credited them with four genocides, although some casino owner will surely disagree.

Slavery was a necessary monument building step. And historians, busy shining seat covers as they generally are, tend to mark monumental [beyond useful] architecture as a sure sign of civilization. In so doing they have tacitly agreed that civilization and slavery are mutually dependent states. In our own postmodern sense, civilization is seen as a condition of ease, luxury and plenty. Before the development of technologies sufficient to replace human labor such a sedentary notion of civilization could only be enjoyed by the few at the expense of the enslaved many.

So, the question is, if the Europeans had not come, would the Iroquois advance from nation to civilization have been made on the backs of Algonquin slaves? If we use the Aztecs, Maya and Incas as models, and consider the Cherokee ownership of black and mixed-race slaves, we will have to answer yes.

I take enough heat for my ambiguity in fiction, so let me stake out a firm opinion. My best answer is that 'nation building' does not require large scale slavery, but that low tech civilizations with monumental architecture and predatory militaries do.

The Roots of Slavery

Slavery begins with mercy, not killing the enemy, or his woman, or his child. Subsistence level societies like the Native Americans of the Eastern Woodlands typically tortured male captives to death, raped and killed the females, and grabbed the children by the feet and smashed their brains out on a tree. If, however, they needed to replace losses, they would enslave the captive and eventually adopt them. To a large degree slavery is something societies without a food surplus could not afford.

Homo Hunterus eats you.

Homo Homocidus kills you.

Homo Surplusses enslaves you.

Homo Industrious hires you, then fires you and lets the corrections system enslave you.

The Faces of Slavery

To take one snapshot of the levels of servitude in the ancient world in the time of the Iliad—you know, Brad Pitt stabbing Eric Bana—I turn to The World of Odysseus by some Brit with an initial for a first name, published by The Folio Society in 2002.

A demioergoi was a servant, who had a contract with his owner, like an apprentice with no human rights.

A dmos was named after the word for house [think domicile], and was owned by a family; the red-headed stepchild of the Iron Age without Charles Dickens to make us weep over his plight.

Lowest of all was the thes, an unattached homeless worker, who was considered wretched by the dmos, who would not change places with his starving ass for all the wine in Ithaca

Later on, in the classical period, the dmos is no longer present, at least not in significant numbers. He has now been replaced by the doulos, who is named after a unit of labor, not the household. As Greek society scaled up chattel slavery was now a reality. Towns emptied as plantations swelled.

The less centralized societies that rose after the fall of Rome could not feed, house, or control armies of slaves. What the Romans did to keep these slaves in line boggles the mind. Feudal lords bound these former slaves to a parcel of land; they and their descendents being organic work units attached to this chunk of dirt for eternity, whoever might come to own it.

Limited forms of slavery included bonding and indenture and gladiatorial servitude, which were 90+% lethal with terms from 3 to 31 years. Technically, most modern soldiers since 1700 have been slaves, un-free men whose officers are armed and authorized to kill them if they decline to kill or attempt to gain their freedom. We, being materialists, think that they are free because they are paid. I remind you, that the gladiators were paid, as were many chattel slaves such as Frederick Douglas and Solomon Northup.

The Effects of Chattel Slavery

Chattel slavery is 100% lethal—nobody gets out alive. This type of slavery is heavily dependent on extreme sociopathic brutality. Every chattel slave was beaten often. Every chattel slave saw a friend or family member executed or beaten to death. The rest were all worked or starved to death. For the past 15 years I have been studying slavery, and I have come up with a worst 10 types of chattel slavery:

1. Roman mine slave [You are not seeing daylight again.]

2. Amerindian mine slave under the conquistadors [What's that guy with the lice in his face hair screaming about—boom!]

3. Roman agricultural slave [All 95 pounds of you.]

4. Islamic eunuch, with 9 of 10 dying immediately from the initial castration—yes that is a better draw of the lots than being one of the three doomed bastards above!

5. Haitian agricultural slave [Broken on the wheel is nastier than it sounds.]

6. Irish Barbados agricultural slave [Death by sunburn.]

7. African American agricultural slave [Yes the guy that owns you is drunk all of the time and his wife is mean as cat shit because she knows he's screwing your mother, and her sister, and your sister, and...]

8. Italian galley slave [Ben Hur, circa 1500, and you're not Chuck Heston so you don't have any teeth to gnaw on that brick they call a biscuit.]

9. Islamic sex slave [They drown your baby in a bucket and then rape you again.]

10. White American agricultural slave [Nobody gives a shit about you boy.]

In the ancient world slavery stifled technology. Archimedes could invent a steam engine every week, but why bother building one when you have 1,000 naked dudes to drag your stuff around? Chattel slavery corrupted the entire civilization wherever it was instituted. Much of history is in fact, the abused mutant child of such savage economies.

Slavery in America

The conquistadors settled the Americas trying to get around the Arab world and hit them in the ass. They aped the Arabs in their methods of enslavement. Unfortunately, 19 out of 20 million Amerindians died in slavery and needed to be replaced. The Africans brought across the Atlantic were a mere trickle compared to those marched across the Sahara as sex slaves to have their penis and testicles chopped off and babies drowned. The vast majority of American slaves went to hell holes like Haiti. Note that many Islamic names indicate that the person so-named is the 'slave' or 'servant' of an aspect of God. The Spaniards who conquered the new world were the sons and grandsons of the men who drove the Muslims from Spain. They seemed to have adopted the Islamic notion of servitude with alarming avarice and unparalleled brutality. The English slavery model seemed to harken right back to ancient Rome.

Roughly a few million went to North America [There is a lot of dispute here. In any case, European slaves abducted and mutilated for the Arab sex trade were roughly equal to those shipped to North America during the 17th and 18th

Centuries.] Also, most female slaves in North America were also sex slaves, and thanks to the outlawing of a mixed race caste, were used as slave breeders by the very men who were abusing them as sex objects, men who gladly enslaved, sold, and killed their own children. Thanks largely to this Southern American Porn Confederacy slave numbers stayed stable and even grew without the massive additional imports required to keep the Caribbean work forces stable. The Brazilians were also race-mixing sex fiends that bred a huge mixed race population, resulting in the best built hip-hop honeys on the rap scene—okay it's not the pyramids, but ought to count for something.

The Superiority of Wage Slavery

After the rich English kicked their serfs and peasants off the land and shipped their children into old Roman style slavery in America, one of these gouty fellows invented the steam engine. Now little English children could be employed as factory slaves, thousands every year fed into the meat-ripping bone-crushing maws of industrial weaving machines. The smart money in America, who were developing their own banking and business models on the European plan, now wanted little Chinese people for the same hideous exploitation. Why own someone when you incur the expense of housing, feeding and guarding them? Find some poor foreign bastard who is small enough to live on scarps and tough enough to live in the open, and put him to work for pennies.

Did the U.S. Need Agricultural Slavery to Compete with Europe?

This is the easy question.

As stated above in the brief on chattel slavery, it is not free, and ultimately stifles economic development beyond anything the Romans or Gauls had in antiquity. The American system began as English slavery, with a brief period in which blacks were imported to hunt escaped white salves. Then the whites were permitted to run off, but could not compete as wage laborers against large plantation gangs, so were employed as slave catchers. It was a cruel system in which the government played off the poor against the slaves for the enrichment of the elite.

The American Civil War was fought to update the American economy to European wage-slavery standards, not to free the slaves, who nobody but Nathan Bedford Forest and a couple of others wanted as a free mobile wage-earning work force. The plan was to strangle the black population, and it worked, with Americans of Africa descent still only 10% of the population. Planned Parenthood was developed to prevent blacks from reproducing in America, and even Lincoln, the 'great emancipator', wanted to ship all of the blacks back to Africa.

America did not become a world class power until a full generation after the end of chattel slavery. A nation cannot build the industry capable of arming and grinding to bloody mud tens of millions of soldiers on the shoulders of a malnourished minority toiling under the same system that barely fed their ancestors 2,000 years ago. It has been argued that the end of American slavery was more beneficial to the northern states than to the European nations. And during the course of that same generation that saw the growth of America into a world class power, the vast majority of former black slaves were reduced to serf status under Jim Crow, even as new waves of wage slaves were brought into the nation as cheap labor so that descendents of former white slaves could be lead to war around the globe by the descendents of former slave owners and aristocrats.

So, essentially America 'caught up' with Europe by abolishing chattel slavery, a type of chattel slavery which was among the cruelest of its kind because it used religion—specifically protestant interpretations of the Old Testament—as a means of justification. As with all chattel systems the legacy of the brutal means necessary to its operation has rippled down through the generations, enabling and excusing senseless violence and wealth redistribution to this very day.

Further Reading

Check out The Slave Trade by Hugh Thomas, The World of Odysseus by M. I. Finley, Hernando de Soto, A Savage Quest in The Americas by David Ewing Duncan, The Truth About Slavery by Stephan Molyneux [he gets the economics, but not the horror, of slavery], and the biography tag on this site.

Also Leah, might I recommend for your students: Gay Rapists of the Caribbean, and Why Grownups

Suck, available on the blog page at jameslafond.com!

-Regal M-116-S

'Really To the Wall'

The Politically Incorrect Extinction Event
Sweepstakes According to Regal M-116-S

© 2014 James LaFond

I must be nearing the end of my longevity, for I have recently begun socializing with humans again, some of whom I am becoming quite fond of. Last night I had a conversation with a reader of mine. We met at a microbrew pub and talked for three hours over as many beers. I was hoping for an assassination attempt as my Harm City page has been barren of late, but this kindly human feted me instead. He brought up what I thought was a very minor documentary review I did on Monday about Google's attempt to scan all of human literature and establish a universal library. Another reader had written in and commented on this brief review, so I was once again blindsided by how something I spent 15 minutes writing could strike such a nerve.

Take Me To Your Breeder

Below I quote Mathis, who I suspect is descended from North African Jewish Berbers [I am an accredited anthropologist you know—well, for me it is zoology]:

"If you would have told me twenty—even ten—years ago, that I would be watching an Aljazeera or goddamned Russian TV documentary , and saying, 'yeah, that's unbiased coverage, how come our American press is so slanted', I would have said, 'Fuck you!' But the sorry fact is that our press is so far into the political pocket that all you have to do to be seditious and question The Empire, is to do objective reporting. The commentators on that documentary I did not find very interesting. They are all equally just commodities. I think you're lucky man—I mean as a writer. Granted I don't know anyone who would want to live like you, surrounded by these soulless hipsters in here and those violent criminals out there. But you are to the wall man; you, Donavon, Nowicki—you guys are writing about the near future like Orwell, and London and those guys did. But they wrote in a time when you could write, that the right to a voiced opinion was considered a bedrock value. Dude, you are ten years from getting shut down. Maybe you will last longer since you have the fiction and the combat and your opinion is buried in all that shit. But guys like Donavon, he had to get out of the workforce and become a tattoo artist just so he could continue to voice his opinion—and that's now. What about tomorrow?"

I reminded him that Fred Reed has been censored by the U.S. government for commenting on military affairs.

"Okay, one down, partway down at least—the elder statesman banned by the establishment. What about the rest of you guys—you being the least known—when does Google or whoever pull the plug, and silence the alternative voices?"

I confided that I do not think it will come to Homeland Security kicking down my door. I do, however, expect that one day, I will log onto the back end and find out that my articles critical of our modern matrix might have been deleted, or to find filters in place that prevent me from using certain words [which initially happened until Charles worked some magic to permit me to use certain proprietary names. I could not post an article that reference prescription drugs, NFL players, etc. and that was just voluntary web host controls.] Granted, my commentary on what I regard as our 'sick society' is not a large part of my work, and is certainly of negligible importance as my readership is tiny and is self-help and fiction oriented.

Below is the list of authors that I expect to be silenced, restricted or killed by the corporate/government/media complex in the next decade in the order in which I think their state-inspired demise is likely:

1. Fred Reed [in progress]

2. Jack Donavon, author of The Way of Men, [they might actually shoot him]

3. Stephan Molyneux, libertarian YouTube talking head [easily frightened by sun-glassed goons I think]

4. Andy Nowicki, author of Lost Violent Souls, [mental health facility here he comes]

5. Peter Joseph [will be bought off with a recording contract]

Fortunately, as a lowly extraterrestrial anthropologist, I am immune to terrestrial persecution, as I have transmigratory properties, and refuse to be held responsible for the caustic ranting of my increasingly decrepit LaFond avatar. Did you know that ever since I permitted this stupid ape to unwisely take up boxing again at age 51 that his nose bleeds constantly? Charles, can I get an upgrade please? There is surely a genius level athlete available somewhere on this overpopulated continent!

The Blight of Spring

An Extraterrestrial View of Your Panhandler Nation

© 2014 James LaFond

Ah, for sweet spring!

The sun is shining.

The sky is clear and blue.

The birds are singing.

Now some vagrant starts harassing you!

The deep dark creviced haunts wherein the human bile of the collective urban digestive tract you humans so witlessly call 'the streets' somehow vomits every April, like a great unsavory bellows, spewing its proto-human contents—that's right, onto my lowly avatar's six-year-old work boots.

Take Me To Your Breeder

This past Sunday, April 13, I am awaiting my massive conveyance, the tube-like land ship that has been thoughtfully staffed with numerous entertainers to occupy my jaunt across town, and to serve as human shields in case of an attempt upon my august person, or as air bags in case my chauffer's skills are found wanting. Granted they have not the social skills I had once come to expect from your kind. Their purpose though, remains.

There I stand, beneath a humming light pole erected in honor of Warlord Eisenhower reading my arcane tome. However, before I might be whisked away like a wizard upon his carpet I am approached from behind by a short stooped Caucasiod ape. He has, in his left hand a large empty gas can, with nozzle. In his right hand he holds the means by which his kind rose from the lesser apes to rule this planet: a lighter, the source of fire! I worriedly consider the lethal implications of the simultaneous use of these two devices. He puts me at ease. I should have known by now—but you humans still baffle me in so many ways—that he is engaged in 'addiction plea behavior'; the ritual groveling practiced by those of your kind who find themselves addicted to this combustible, or that injectible, or one of your many brain-eating liquid ingestibles.

He begs a cigarette, and I have none with which to placate him. He then requests currency with which he might purchase cigarettes, and I plead poverty, something I reason he is equipped to comprehend. I breathe my own apish sigh of relief as he moves off down the concrete footpath.

I notice him squatting on his haunches down the way, before the altar of your petroleum god—having used a credit card to access the church database—and is now filling his gas can with a substance so flammable that I once advised the Hierarch of Constantinople to use it against the besieging Arab fleet—to hideous effect, I might add. From this distance this is all I can make out, as my LaFond avatar's optics are steadily failing.

This creature has now been joined by a tall lanky member of his begrimed pack and they begin to move in my direction. When they are twenty feet away the short fellow procures a cigarette butt from the gutter, puts it to his bristly lip as he cradles his sloshing gas can, and lights the noxious stub with his lighter. I then experience a number of taut moments as he and his hairy fellow walk by, him with a lit object between the fingers of his right hand and a few gallons of gasoline in the red container in his left hand. I now more fully appreciate the sacrifices made by my colleague Jane when she studied the Chimpanzees of Gombo. If I recall correctly one of her apes toted a gas can around as well, to enhance his status I think.

Then my chugging chariot arrives.

On assignment, Regal M-116-S

Earth Station Estrogen

A Book Store Clerk Asks the Extraterrestrial
Anthropologist about Her Gender's Past Plight

© 2014 James LaFond

Have you ever experienced that 'rock star'
moment?

I have only had said opportunity when engaged in
my research at libraries and book stores. Such
occasions to savor my dubious celebrity status are
then generally ruined when the combined thickness
of mine and the book curator's glasses render
meaningful eye contact impossible. Never-the-less, I
am not one to deny a reader's request to access the
vast database housed between these attentive ears,
particularly when she, well, when she is a she.

The Question

Josey Thomas, 21st Century Human Female, asked me [that would be Regal M-116-S, toiling away under the stifling conditions of this research grant—can I not deploy the nanobots at least once a millennium!]:

"At what time in history, before the 21st Century, was it ever 'great' to be a woman?"

By implication Josey regards the plight of current females in her experimental habitat, known as 21st Century America, to be enjoying a 'great' life. I would concur. Thus far, if one were to choose to be born in any time in human experience, as a random, median female, than 21st Century America would be the five-star destination.

I will further focus the question in terms of gender equity, which was the subject upon which Josey and I were discoursing. Permit me Josey, to reframe the question.

"At what time-and-place in the human experience, excepting the post women's suffrage era in the West, has a woman's lot been socially,

physically, morally, and materially equal to, or preferable to, the lot of her male counterpart?'

The Human Gender Paradigm

First off, You People [As an alien zoologist I can say that.] are quite literally screwed by the whole sexual reproduction model of propagation. In fact, in your own best interest, I actually took a pilgrimage in human form to meet with your Designer. I know, some of you think he is a shattered singularity, and others that he resides on a cloudbank mysteriously unperturbed by airline traffic. Regardless I found him in 1981, sitting on a milk crate above a drainage ditch, behind a food market, in Northeast Baltimore. He did assure me that he was your Designer, and that he was mighty upset with how things were turning out with his planet. He was a huge man, smelled much like John the Baptist must have, and proved his supernatural powers by breaking a pallet over his knee. There was no combusting shrub in sight, but he did assure me that he could fry a hamburger under the hole in the ozone layer caused by the Freon leaking from the transformer that powered the frozen food case that my LaFond avatar was toiling to fill daily in his pathetic life-long service to my—but I digress.

104

Here it is in a 'nutshell', as your primordial ancestors must have thought, Josey.

You are just fragile little apes on a planet of canines, felines, bovines, etc. You need a ruthless half to go out and kill all of these hairy brutes, and a compliant half that is going to bend over for the most ruthless and then put up with the screaming and defecating of his resulting progeny. He kills 'them', then impregnates 'you' with that nasty little ape that is going to kill the next generation of 'them'.

Now Josey, do you now more clearly understand my preference for transmigratory reproduction? Examine and consider the process above, which is the process by which your Designer [who I suspect had some issues—you should have seen how he went after that poor pallet!] apparently intended you to thrive. Really, if you were a feline, or particularly a bovine, and were to witness a nature film whereby the human male is shown impregnating the female [nasty business that is], then the female is seen painfully ejecting the little hominid from her belly, then through time-lapse effect we are treated to scenes of the male young attacking progressively larger prey from toy reptile, to house cat, to domestic dog, and then finally taking up his high-powered rifle and six-pack of beer to go kill skittish ungulates in rough wooded terrain, then you might feel a bit like Sigourney Weaver in any of her Aliens roles.

So Josey, taking into account that you were designed to be contested property, to be grappled and injected by the hairy killer that acquires you, you have indeed come a long way. Your species design, my dear, begs for coercion, and being the vessel of the next generation of habitat exploiters does tend to put the female half into an objectified social cul-de-sac. Next I shall address your enemy within.

Of Queens and Wenches

We must be careful, when considering the typical woman's lot in life, not to wax too nostalgic about the queens of ages past. Think of the last 'queen' you worked with. As with any life form which claws its way up out of a situational cul-de-sac, a successful woman is very unlikely to extend a helping hand to those whose persons she just used as stepping stones in her ascent. Throughout history powerful women have been noted for their hatred of and cruelty toward less fortunate women.

This is particularly prominent when a powerful woman's position is due to her status as highly valued sexual property. In this light, the worst situation to be born into is as a female slave to a rich woman, who is only rich because she is the slave of a powerful man.

Keeping in mind that man's power over woman is vested in his proficiency with violent means we shall consider prominent violent women as one sign of endemic social mobility for women within a society. Women are, we must remember, the half of this volatile human species that resides 'within' its groups, generally with little intercourse outside the group, except as an object of value. Therefore, prominence of women in war or other means of dealing with outside groups is indicative of women enjoying greater equity with men in that culture than has generally been common.

Josey's Time-Place Holiday Menu

Now Josey supposing we had a time-place machine that could whisk you away to the past at a certain place, I have listed for you the occupation among the people in question that best expresses the greater status of women in that society than has been the human norm. This will not necessarily be the typical lot of a woman in said society. However, we might suppose that my patronage as an extraterrestrial dignitary would gain you access to this occupation. As I have never chosen to transmigrate into the body of a female fetus upon the expiration of my various avatars [although, when this LaFond unit hits the floor for good I might alter this arrangement, considering the way things are going among you humans] I will make no attempt to rate these favorable female plights.

Favorable Female Plights

The time-place destinations are divided by body type. Just as a male time traveler who weighed 90 pounds would not want to go back to 9th Century Norway, a petite woman would be best advised to avoid the Stone Age options.

Fat Girl Destinations

Josey, do not go back as a fashion model before A. D. 1600!

Bubble Butt Copoid Nomad

Your best bet is to go back about 40,000 years to the drier climates in Africa and Iberia where the 'copoid' people once roamed. Alone among humans you would have enhanced labial tissue and an extra 'rumble seat' for additional fat storage. You would be the primordial hip hop honey, valued a great deal by your men, who have been noted for being non-warlike. The downside is that your men all got slaughtered by the whites and the blacks after the invention of iron. It is likely that the African man's obsession with large butts stems from 40 plus millennia of annihilating little copper-skinned dudes and appropriating their light-skinned bubble butt babes. You want to go early, or at least before the prehistoric equivalent of the NBA invent iron spearheads and goes on the warpath.

Paleolithic Sex Goddess

A feminist once wrote a book titled, When God Was Woman. If I wrote that book it would be titled, When White Guys Liked Fat Chicks! Fresh steak on the grille every day Josey! Sure, it was awful damned cold in Ice Age Europe. But every hunter in the band will be seeking your—well not exactly your hand at this stage in human evolution—and be out there slaughtering animals so big and hairy that your fur coat would break Jennifer Anniston's back, and the rack of ribs your old man—if he still wants to be your old man—brings home could easily tip over Fred Flintstone's foot-powered car at the Bedrock Diner! To be the prehistoric Marilyn Monroe all you have to do is sew, keep the fire stoked, haul your house around in pieces [you might want to invest in a few sisters] and maintain huge breasts, a big belly and a fat butt. You've got to keep an eye on your old man though. He's sniffing around upriver after those redheads.

Neanderthal Wet Nurse

Based on the size of their heads Neanderthal children needed longer periods of care under their mother than other humans. Your correspondingly low birthrate compared to those tall skinny wives-of-murderers downriver does put you at an evolutionary disadvantage. Also, the fact that your muscle bound men cannot throw weapons but must get inside and stab, and no smartass has invented the bow and arrow yet, has them taking too many casualties hunting and makes them outnumbered sitting ducks against the invading bone-racks. The upside is, those skinny dudes that murder your men every time they get caught out in the open, 'like big butts', and you've got that going on girlfriend. You want to be a Neanderthal babe before 40,000 years ago. Most of your people will be murdered and raped by those bone-racks between 35,000 and 27,000 years ago, leaving a 2% trace Neanderthal DNA in the modern human genome. I'm guessing there aren't a lot of Neanderthal paternal markers, so don't get too attached to your son if your time-place machine stalls out this side of 33,000 B.C.

Ugandan Beauty Queen

If you go back to pre-colonial Uganda, and have a large enough frame to get immensely fat, than you can drink milk all day long, have gangs of skinny girls lotion your skin while male slaves turn you over so you don't get bed sores, and be an actual—if not very mobile—beauty queen.

Little Girl Destinations

In any society the accepted body image for women has much bearing on the actual status of individual females. Little girl time-place occupations have more to do with doing than being. Lazy urban women beware.

Native American Interpreter

The relative plasticity of female language skills had important applications for the advanced stone aged peoples of North and South America. While there were some matriarchal Amerindian societies, most were patriarchal. However, the vast variety of languages due to the small scale societies of these vast wildernesses made the interpreter invaluable. The female interpreter became even more valuable when the Whites came. So when the apocalyptic shit hits the fan your stock soars. Many Native women married trappers and combined the interpreter role with that of mobile house manager and enjoyed actual 50/50 partnership arrangements with these White men, who were very lonely and under actual diplomatic pressure to treat their Native wives good.

Iroquoian Housewife

Relax! It's a big house, a long one actually, and you don't have to clean it yourself because you live with your sisters, each with your own apartment. You own everything in it and get to vote! The only thing your husband owns is his weapons, and he is away half the year wiping our rivals from the cousin or alien tribes. You do work outside the home in your gardens, and the senior women basically run the towns. Your men are the most feared warriors in this land, because you are such a nagging bitch that he can't stand to stay home and goes raiding for hundreds of miles around. The Whites fear your men and make deals with them, meaning you get a lot of good White People tools and nic-nacs for your nice warm house. When your warriors bring home captives, you even get to torture and kill them in case you woke up on the wrong side of the bed— and you actually have a bed! In what became the Carolinas there was even a woman, the Princess of Cafitachequi, who headed a confederation of towns.

Spartan Woman

A woman of Sparta managed the property—including the slaves—and came of age playing sports, largely in the company of other girls. Her older female relatives selected a husband for her. She was important because she was a breeder of warriors. So if you are terrified of pregnancy and can't stand boys under the age of seven, find another gig. No woman had a better life in the Greco-Roman world than a Spartan wife. Not only did she not get pregnant as soon as physically possible as in most other societies, she was in better health. And, as an added bonus, when she was too old to have children, she served as a sexual instructor for the 20-year old men. If you like the idea of teaching a squad of young soldiers how to have intercourse, then being a 45-year-old Spartan woman sounds a lot like a middle-aged woman's version of a modern American college girl's trip to Cancun. I guess at this point, you realize that you want to be on good terms with your aunt, because she is the chick that's breaking in the young guys and recommending one as your husband.

Hellenistic Philosopher

There was at least one notable female philosopher
from the 200s B.C. The era was one in which many
atheistic notions were entertained, and
motherhood was not regarded as paramount for a
woman by certain affluent communities who hired
mercenary soldiers. This was a blink of the macro-
cultural eye, and seems to have been similar in
some ways to our age of change and angst. Don't
leave any daughters behind for the Romans.

Scythian Amazon

Don't get too attached to your right breast, because
it needs to come off! Yep, as long as you can ride
and shoot a composite bow, you're a man with the
ability to have children. You will give up any boys to
be adopted by the men, and keep the girls to be
raised as female warriors.

These women were the inspiration for the Greek
legend of the Amazons. Gene Wolfe in Soldier of
Arete, and Steven Pressfield in Last of the Amazons,
did nice fictional renderings of this half-mythic

culture. We know the Scythians had female warriors, and chiefs. I doubt if they were all Amazons, but the existence of a female warrior society among them speaks volumes for their gender equity situation. These were Caucasian nomads. Later Asian nomads had a less extreme tolerance for female leadership.

Nordic Battleaxe

If you are big, bitchy, and sexy than any number of Celtic and Germanic pagan societies would provide a sensibly assertive woman avenues for a better standard of living and limited autonomy, **if** she hooked up with the right man. One particular she-devil took over the last expedition to Vinland and scared the death out of the Natives by beating her naked breast with a sword. The Roman writer Tacitus complained a thousand years earlier that there was a tribe of Germans who actually tolerated female opinions! Celtic and German women sometimes earned the right to fight alongside their husbands. Famously, Boudicca, in A. D. 73 had enough clout to convince tens of thousands of fellow Breton men to throw away their lives battling the Roman legions.

Pre-Islamic Berber Woman

The semi-nomadic people of Northwest Africa famously resisted Muslim invaders under a queen. There is reason to believe that at some time before A.D. 600 that a culture of limited political tolerance for women was thriving in his area. It probably would not seem like equity to a modern American woman. But to a modern Muslim woman, or for most women throughout history, it would be a liberated life, if it produced a warrior queen who men were willing to fight for against men who held women as veiled property. The women of this region, as late as the early 1900s, were hated and feared by men of the French Foreign Legion, who, if captured, would be given to the women to torture.

Dahomey Amazon

You get to have sex with the king, push men around, belong to an elite military unit, and even marry a woman who can raise that baby that result from His Majesty's kingly attention. I realize that this option

117

is more for the ghetto girls. But I had to put something low rent on the itinerary Josey.

I hope this helps.

Extraterrestrially Yours, Regal M-116-S

Prisoner of The Apes

A Reluctant Earthling's Guide to Human History

© 2014 James LaFond

I have recently been quizzed by two of your more pleasing females as to my political thoughts and leanings. This is ironic, that those who I am, as an extraterrestrial anthropologist, barred from mating with, might inquire of me as to that other human pursuit—namely mass violence—that I am also barred from engaging in. These zoological research grants do have such nagging stipulations.

What follows is a brief outline of human history, which is to say politics. Politics is the act of banding into groups in order to do violence to individuals and groups, or to preserve one's self and fellow from said violence. This is not typically understood for what it is. I have known three types of earthlings, politically speaking, and will describe them according to the frequency with which they appear.

Gatherer/Farmer/Collectivist

Collectivists are defined by a need for security and a grasping materialism, or concern with material comforts: doubtlessly harkening back to the ape's need for a comfortable tree to cling to as the four-legs prowled the forest floor below. Virtually all females are, by nature, collectivist. Most males, typically lacking the means to violently overcome their fellow, are also, by nature, collectivists. Collectivists are controlled most easily through horizontal social pressure. The psychological characteristic of the collectivist is that they do not understand the mechanics of violence, specifically the nuance of threat. You are descended from skittish tree-grazing monkey-men to put it bluntly. It is not surprising therefore that 7 in 10 of your males and better than 9 in 10 of your females are incapable of consistently and effectively understanding, using, or resisting violent means. Indeed it is a miracle that you creatures ever got out of the trees.

Your history is therefore a litany of 'great men', violent little apes, who have imposed their will and therefore advanced the cause of others like themselves, who would successively harness the collectivist impulse to support and amplify their violent actions down through the bloody ages. Somewhere, in deep prehistory, is a hairy little Napoleon with a sharp rock.

In humans the collectivist impulse probably came down through the fear of leopards, which is ingrained in primates. In fact, were it not for prehistoric hominids being killed by leopards, we would have scarce evidence of their existence, as leopards take their kills to secluded and sheltered locations, providing zoologists—I'm sorry, anthropologists—like myself fossils nicely preserved from erosion.

The intensification of this impulse to gather round the fire and fend off the big cat was eventually turned outward toward hyena, lion and baboon, and every other creature fated to share this world with you little monsters, and ultimately upon other groups of apes. We do have a charming example from some millions of years ago left by your nasty little ancestors in the form of an entire troop of baboons who had been murdered with rocks. After investigating that mess I have never again looked upon a baseball game as quaint.

As the term applies, the gathering, or 'collecting' portion of the hunter-gatherer lifeway encourages passive group cohesion just as the hunting aspect encourages lethal group cohesion. So, when the advent of agriculture, of actually cooperating with the plants you fed on, came about, it revolutionized human life. The immediate result was the concentration of wealth in the hands of the few, and the enjoyment for those few, of a progressively better standard of living. Actual human history as studied by your historians is a study of these fortunate few at the top of the collectivist heap at the expense of their slaves, by a margin of better than 1,000 books to one. The corollary was the wretched lot of the farmer, which would provide most of humanity 6,000 years of miserably impoverished toil, with life spans no longer than that of the hominid shivering in fear of the leopard. The difference was that the human farmer shivered in fear of something else; another hunter, who had evolved on a parallel and intersecting track—and so did his master fear him as well.

Hunter/Herder/Politician

The killing of progressively larger and more numerous animals makes for a much more effective combatant than digging for roots. A good recent example is the famed Mountain Man 'Liver-Eating' Johnson, who killed more Native Americans than General George Armstrong Custer and his entire 7th Cavalry. This was common for Mountain Men, many of whom had dozens of human kills, it being an extension of their trade, which was the killing of large dangerous animals. Being renowned as the most prolific 'Injun' killer, the cannibal warrior Johnson was once asked about his tally of foes. He declined to count the 'digger Injuns' he had killed, as they were not hunters.

While the collecting of plants led to their cultivation, the hunting of animals led to their domestication. This act of herding is even more predatory on a social level than hunting, as the herd animal is subject to sub-lethal coercion, encouraged into predictable behavior patterns, and finally rounded up and slain en masse. Throughout history, until the Russian Czars finally broke the Mongol yoke, Eurasian military history was little more than a litany of barbarian invasions by cattle herding people, followed by long intervals in which the descendents of these invaders ruled the farming societies. In Africa the cattle herding Bantu peoples likewise terrorized more sedentary cultivators. In the New World the famed Aztecs, who actually ate those who opposed their 'gods', were descendents of a 'Dog People', a group of savage nomads.

The skill of the herder in convincing his doomed domestic beast that the herder is his friend and provider, and cannot thus be dispensed with, is at once the root of and mechanism by which massive modern populations are controlled. You skittish little apes do not even know you live under threat; indeed are intelligent enough to rationalize this process as something other than a threat matrix leading to your digestion by successive generations of your masters.

Exile/Criminal/Individualist

The ancient method for dealing with aberrant and seditious persons was exile. This process in a global society is more or less internal, with passive nonconformists enjoying less privilege—very often as a homeless man. Passive non-conformists in modern America are almost all homeless males.

Aggressive non-conformists can best be illustrated by referring back to the Mountain Men of the 19th Century American West. Numbering no more than a hundred at any given time, these men had rejected civilization. They lived in the primal hunting sphere of the Native Americans, as individuals. A rough average of 10 human kills was required for these men to maintain their personal autonomy over the course of what was usually a mere two decades of such living, often resulting in a violent death. This perilous and most free form of individualist life was made possible by four factors:

1. Violent means, with all of these men being effective killers on the order of a modern special warfare soldier with a sniper or hand-to-hand specialty.

2. Alliances with as many Native American tribes as one was at war with

3. A voluntary reciprocal complex in which these individuals pledged assistance to one another. They did not band together for protection, but rather banded together for vengeance when one of their lonely kind was killed, robbed or dishonored by a band, tribe or nation. Liver-Eater Johnson was

elected to lead at least three of these mini genocidal expeditions.

4. The absence of a federating macroparasitic entity. To the extent that the Mountain Men continued their ways after the U.S. gained control of these lands, they did so as criminals. Johnson was reprimanded for taking Cherokee scalps when serving with the Union Cavalry in Missouri. A friend of his was eventually killed by a posse of Latino fighters, bringing to an end his decades of abducting 'wives' from that community [He did return them unharmed when he got sick of them]. In our day and age, the men who understand that autonomy has only been had by violent means, either ply violence on behalf of the state [police/military] as Johnson sometimes did, or ply it in the shadows of the collective, alone or alongside temporary allies, as criminals, as Johnson usually did. The 21st Century American corollary to the Mountain Man—who enjoyed more autonomy than perhaps any humans that ever lived, at the cost of great hardship—is the urban gang set player, who likewise has a famously short, if colorful, life.

Charming Non-Violent Individualists

Personally speaking, as a collector of futuristic ideas an interesting development is the exploration by some of the brighter passive dissidents among you of anarchist/libertarian models for non-violent autonomous human interaction. Now, you are not only my favorite life form, but the subject of my doctoral thesis as well, so I would like to see humans colonizing the moons, the planets and distant worlds—just not in the Regal System thank you!

So, it is interesting to wonder if there is a way that humanity can exist without constant threat of, and implementation of, lethal force. Thus far, I have found no evidence that this has ever been the case. And as far as the increased lethality of force down through the ages, the corollary development has been, well, the air conditioner. If you renounced forcing and killing one another, the evidence suggests that technology would wither.

And if this came to pass, how would I be able to keep cool during your torrid summers?

Would you libertarians agree to take turns fanning me?

Or would I have to break open my aerosol contingency canister and 'make of your daughter a slave' as one of your more notable autonomous males of ancient times once warned?

Violent Greedy Apes

The human condition itself is defined by the grasping materialism of the collective female impulse—gather those nuts and thatch that nest baby—amplified by the predatory male hunting complex—dude, it's just a cave! What could go wrong?

Throughout most of human history the collectivist impulse has served the hunter's need as expressed by the apex human predator, the military-backed politician, who occupies most of the pages of your history books. Although many a million little ape has died horribly in the process this does appear to be a symbiotic relationship, with the vast collective typically content that the force wielded by its ruling class is wielded in its name, for its own collective good. Besides, you are still multiplying, objective proof that your violent politicians have been right all along.

Although I am far from an economist, I suppose the extent to which it is true that living collectively under protection of a military force is a progressive act, could be proven by a natural increase in the material wealth of the collective masses and a reduction in the material wealth of the ruling class—you know, like when Genghis Khan, Liver-Eating Johnson, and other mass-murdering nomad leaders gave most of their wealth away.

-Regal M-116-S

Below the Social Horizon

Field Notes from an Extraterrestrial Anthropologist

© 2014 James LaFond

As a visiting zoologist—I'm sorry, anthropologist—it is incumbent upon me to refrain from involvement in your aggression sequencing behaviors. When I'm done my work with documenting your first phase—really, you are not so far along as you seem to think—then I shall be recalled, and hopefully permitted to reproduce back on Regal. I'll be replaced by the military R&D geek squad who will determine how best to weaponize you. I'm no expert, but I think tossing the entire planet load of you little beasties at Sirius would go a long way towards evening that particular score.

No Charles, I am not afraid of being recalled for running on at the information orifice. I'm hoping it will happen at this point. You people are beginning to scare me. Below are some facts concerning the aggression suite you people of Blue—why do you call it Dirt?—refer to as 'the economy'.

1. While investigating your prurient proclivities [it is one of my necessary sub-routines I'll have you know] via a Vice video concerning the 300-plus thriving strip clubs in the gluteal augmentation capital of the world, otherwise known as Atlanta Georgia, one of the strip club owners stated that owning a strip club was a smart business decision during an economic 'depression'! This dumb earthling actually used that term! Your Minister of Finance should have him—oh yes, that brings us to #2...

2. Your Dark Lord's Supreme Court just upheld the right of the U.S. federal government to detain U.S. citizens indefinitely, without charges, under the NDAA.

3. English professor and sci-fi and social commentary author Andy Nowicki is one step closer to experiencing that NDAA guideline, as he is being targeted for removal from his higher education post based on the content of his

published literature [mostly about depressed American men contemplating the meaning of life].

4. Your Dark Lord and his rather pale Lord of the Nazgul just spent 40 million dollars on a vacation, thereby comforting me with the hope that, after a few more generations, your world leaders will once again be as much fun to party with as Caligula.

5. The Generals of Your Dark Lord's orkish hordes have just entered into an agreement which will permit his minions to operate out of 5 Filipino military bases, which does make my news viewing more interesting. Africa is already boring me—oh yes.

6. Nigerian slave girls are once again being sold to Muslim men in that fine nation. Ah, but for tradition where would we be?

7. The striking young lady who was the CEO of Bitcoin supposedly committed suicide by throwing herself off a balcony in Singapore, where, last year, a young American man working for another multinational was also determined by the sterling Singapore police to have committed suicide in the flower of his youth.

8. Closer to home, the EPA is permitting DOW to spray an upgraded version of 'Agent Orange' that goes by the charming name of 2, 4-D, on its crops of genetically engineered soybeans and corn. Yum!

9. Finally, on the upside, 12 investment bankers have committed suicide thus far, merely a third of the way through the 2014th year of your rather imaginative Lord.

That is it, nine unconnected factoids. Please don't use them to bind any kings in the darkness.

Regal M-116-S

The Great Camel Trade of 2014

An Exclusive Extraterrestrial OP/ED on The Capitalist Caliph's Master Stroke

© 2014 James LaFond

Greetings Earthlings: Regal M-116-S here. Presently I am quite bored with your publicized social functions, and it is against my Prime Directive to read the minds of your leaders and expose their prurient thoughts concerning Brangalina to your huddled masses. On the other hand, Charles has yet to provide me with that plane ticket that will enable me to journey to Hawaii to observe that hula dancing ritual I have heard so much of...

So, I found myself fallen from academic grace once again as I actually subjected myself to the viewing of your network news. It was not all so bad. After all, the adorable little creature that owns that particularly large TV was perched upon what would be my knee if I were not limbed after the reticulated manner fashionable back on Regal, and was complying with my margarita requests most promptly. Hence I saw no need to critique her information tastes. Information is not, after all, her purpose.

Then came the news on all five networks, about the great swapping of a badminton playing deserter from your besieged and evaporating army, who was apparently such a bore that your Taliban enemies—not exactly a band of Joe Rogan imitators themselves—decided to part with him rather than parting him from his head, which I believe is their preferred form of diplomacy.

Not to disparage the fellow, but as I saw him blinking away what remained of his five year high, he appeared to be quite a harmless boy. I know I am no soldier; however, I breakfasted with Baybars, lunched with Vlad Tepes [after disconnecting my olfactory glands mind you], and supped with Cortez as his hounds supped on Aztecs. Also, might I point out that I have survived for thousands of years on your nasty little planet, which is the equivalent of one of your terrestrial educators surviving a weekend on a Detroit street corner! My point is, I know a dangerous human when I see one, and this fellow would not even be regarded as a bait human on Sirius—I have warned you about those people should they come knocking—and is certainly no fighting stud.

Then, to my darling's horror—she is American you know—the TV screen came alive with the faces of five furious fiends from some monotheistic battlefield. Why they appeared a match for any band of movie villains. My alcohol vector blurted, "You mean he traded that pasty faced kid for those five killers! What is up with that?"

And so I was called on again, in my capacity as advisor to human kind, and responded as recorded below—with a sonorous and sage-like tone mind you, "Oh child, this is a 'cunning camel trade' as old Tamerlane once said after bagging the Ottoman Sultan not far from the spot this trade was conducted. Look there, you see that brown fellow of yours: the willowy orator—oh there have been so many—Oh yes, Caliph O'Sauron, your Dark Lord. He is taking quite a bit of temperature at home over his human repairing pyramid scheme, understandably so, as you people have not yet mastered transmigration. You are all in an uproar over the fate of your corporeal forms, prone to malfunction as they are. Believe me, I know. This LaFond avatar is creaking already—can't even get it up to half speed without it wheezing to a stop...

"Yes, in any case, this Dark Lord of yours knows that he must pave the way for his successor, probably that bloodthirsty little female who was married to King William the Fornicator. There is no better mood for the demos to greet the ascension of such a savage little monarch than war fever. How is one to make the nation eager for more decades of a war?

"Make them feel as if their good-meaning leader was duped into exchanging their badminton player for the enemy's five machinegun toting martyrs! Even the opposition party is calling for the rattling of whatever passes for a national saber these days in the matter of the Russian strong man. They will now demand more killing of these pesky goatherds, and the dignified Caliph will drag his feet, to make way for the Mother of War as she will surely one day be called. Just think of how startling the news casts will be then!

"Beyond all of that is the matter of perpetuation. Empires must have continuous war to survive—the old grow or die axiom. Your Caliph's drones rain down death upon women and children and ambulance drivers in order to draw more jihadists into this global war—which is not too terribly easy to prosecute from the back of a donkey, or even those SUVs—and boost military contracts. Every new enemy fighter sparks a mote of fear in the millions of American eyes that reflect from these countless TV screens. That glimmer of fear, My Dear, is the stuff nations are built upon...

"Oh yes, the Jeopardy show will be fine, thank you. And an extra shot of tequila please. We must make it fair for old Alex you know..."

Regal M-116-S Speaks

An Extraterrestrial Anthropologist on WWIII

© 2014 James LaFond

I have been exchanging emails with a young human concerning his nation's war entanglements. Below is one of my missives. This is actually the subject of my ongoing project 40,000 Years from Home, so I will be attaching this as an end note. My next entry for the book will be an interlude on the function of ideology in war: Scalp, Cross, and 401K.

Of course Islam has its infighting. And when fighting an ideological war one must whack all traitors.

How are they winning?

They have already turned the US into a police state. Now it has willingly become that which they claimed it was, with no values in terms of liberty to defend; and that, that liberty impulse is the only thing which has ever broken the chains of faith—game over here. They never have to land. You just need to believe they might. Done deal; 911 was the one punch KO of the moral principal that underpins the materialistic enemy of the caliphate.

The front the 19th Century Islamists had on their mind was Black Africa. Did you know that last year the US conducted operations in 45 African nations? Did you know that in every one of those nations about which I have been able to find reports Black animists, Christians, and secular forces have lost ground to Islamists both black and Arabic? Right now Kenya and Nigeria make the news sometimes. These are the places where what Americans fear will happen here is happening, so reports are filtered.

Let us not forget that this is a religious movement. Only the idea has to cross the border. That is why Homeland Security is buying armored fighting vehicles and many police departments train their officers to confiscate all weapons—even if licensed, legally held and safely stored—that they come across in traffic stops, home investigations, etc. As the US military looses 45 Vietnams in Africa the lessons learned are being brought home by the mercenaries who work for the DOD and passed on to the FBI and Homeland Security who train local police.

The idea is, once Islam blooms in America in the fertile soil of a purely material and deteriorating ideology, the police state should be so centralized as to make it vulnerable to regional insurgencies as has been the case in Afghanistan, which models nicely for an ethnically and ideologically fractured America. Think about it, in a world of the spirit, Afghanistan is the iconic symbol: both the atheist Soviet Union and the materialist US Imperium broke their teeth there. The how and the why is not only not forgotten, but forms the basis for a curriculum taught to boys around the world even as our masters bomb funerals, weddings, and homes and even send drones after the responding ambulance, for a whopping 98% collateral damage tally, further enhancing recruitment of Jihadists from the remaining orphans and embittered survivors.

We have a 4-year view.

The Islamists think in terms of Ages, and will fight for hundreds of years. Western societies have rarely been able to sustain war efforts beyond a decade, and when they have, it has brought about the demise of those societies, the 30 years war being the best case study.

I predict an Islamist win late in this century. Please tell your grandchildren you knew the nut that made the call.

There you have it earthlings. I just don't see the currency of the western banks that provide the means to pay for the West's mercenary forces rising. I do see Islamist currency rising. Today's western militaries are very much analogous to the forces that Wallenstein managed on behalf of this prince and that in the 30 Years War. Even at his apex he never would have dreamed of testing his conglomeration of short term contractors against the will of Islamic arms.

The reason for western hegemony has been superior technology. But now that technology has made the very battlefield obsolete. With war now increasingly a test of societal will and the West refusing to acknowledge the ideological nature of the struggle, I see no other logical conclusion, other than to honor the many American Indian leaders who predicted that although they could not stand before the God of Things, that no purely material society would remain dominant or prosperous for long. Of course, for an American 4 years is forever, so I suppose all of you humans are correct in your own fractious way.

Take Me to Your Breeder

An Extraterrestrial Anthropologist on The Man

© 2014 James LaFond

Good morning humans. This is Regal M-116-S here, subjected to the harsh light of your effervescent dwarf star, and thereby compelled to 'rise and opine'.

Oh my, apologies, wrong apes.

Sorry again, about that reference to your primate propensity to be enamored and rendered witless by shining things; which further beckons me to digress and apologize for inaugurating the shinny bead trade. But what—particularly on earth—is a zoologist—sorry, anthropologist—to do when a pack of savage little apes mistake his carnelian skin for the hide of some mythic beast prone to horde shinny baubles, but to introduce one's evolved self to the primitives through dispensing with any thought of a return to Regal and dismantling the touch nodes of the control module, and thereby dispersing the means of my eventual egress for the purpose of immediate salvation?

Yes, yes, you have me. There is no orbital egress pod. Charles merely maintains my pathetic attempt at building one. I might have mentioned before that I failed my math exam and was thereby shunted off to the zoological corps. I am marooned, and, with your breeding finally unchecked by natural forces, there are few reclusive options. So I occupy myself with the study of the one sentient species with more sorrows than my own—you hairy little fellows!

Yes friends, welcome down out of the trees—just in time it would seem, for they are falling fast...

Hidden Colors 3

I was recently viewing a documentary film by a very well dressed human filmmaker Tariq Nasheed [and if it was not his film it should have been] by King Flex Films. This film was given to me by a young man of color who is studying the plight of his ancestors. He was concerned that the film was propagandistic and did not present supporting evidence for certain authoritative statements given.

Thank you, young human, for this video. I found it very enjoyable. I will limit my comments to three categories: overall impressions, contradictions within the film, and those points made by the 'black separatist' filmmaker, which are in precise agreement with points made by 'white separatist' academics and propagandists, including the extant followers of a certain nasty little mustachioed Austrian of conflicted descent.

'From Coon to Tycoon'

First, I recommend that all humans view this film, keeping in mind that it is a militant race-based call to political, spiritual and economic action. There are many interesting tidbits that are only touched on, such as organ harvesting, secret lynching in today's American South and various conspiracy theories, for which no evidence is presented, but rather taken for well-established fact.

I wish that the history of castration in America was covered in more detail. I loved the segment on George Washington's false teeth being yanked from the mouths of moaning black slaves! The black superman mythology is something that I am very interested in and wish they had gone into greater detail about.

The lady commentator with the light skin and beige queen hat seemed to be a Nation of Islam conspiracy buff, and almost stole the film from Umar Johnson. I know she had to have mentioned Big-headed Yakub, and am quite miffed at Mister Nasheed for cutting that quote from the film.

Do not come to this film expecting to find an illumination of the assertions that are made. This is perhaps the closest parallel between this effort and those of the various veiled white supremacist organizations that call themselves nationalists, separatists and tribal identity groups. Hidden Colors 3 utilizes a number of compelling speakers and a very smooth narrative presentation targeting the adolescent Urban American human according to the art of demagoguery. This film is an example of the art of the eloquent half-truth which has propped up cult leaders and politicians for ages.

Hidden Colors 3 is targeted exclusively at the African American, and artfully conspires to convince him that he is a member of the true master race who 'has the power of extinction' in his very reproductive organs, and that he is therefore hated and set upon by all of the other races of men, including the baleful Europeans and current African immigrants.

Hidden Colors 3 utilizes the ideological alienation techniques favored by police states throughout history, through multiple calls to 'marginalize' any people of African ancestry who get too cozy with the primary enemy, which is 'the whites'. As one of the expert commentators mentions, the material rewards of betraying your black brothers are great, as illustrated in his saying 'from coon to tycoon'.

The best portion of the early half of the film is a cartoon narrated by Tariq Nasheed that correctly depicts the plight of the African America man from the perspective of his uniquely and porously insulated culture. This is where the film works. If you are an American of African ancestry this is the hook that drags you into the net of half truths with open but blinkered eyes. If you are a member of the target audience's genetic enemies than the fact that you have experienced some of these same 'uniquely black' negatives will drive you to click off the video so that you will not be in a position to know what half truths and lies are about to be fed to your darker-skinned fellows. This is the genius stroke: alienating sympathetic views that might contradict some of the militant dogma from the discussion, and, at the same time connecting on an experiential level with the recruit.

The propagandistic aspect of Hidden Colors 3 which most effectively demonstrates the film's nature and mission as an inflammatory rather than an informatory effort, is the fact that the speaker with the most face time is Doctor Umar Johnson, who speaks with wild bugged eyes and expressive hand motions and excited diction in a charmingly ebonic reinterpretation of Adolf Hitler's oratory style. Have you ever viewed a Hitler speech, and wondered to yourself, "How could a nation follow such a nut? Would not a people want a cool-headed leader?"

Not a people who has suffered and who maintains a self-image of oppressive sacrifice at the hands of a greater polity. You see, while most people who view or listen to Hitler or Johnson flex and rant and posture are repelled by the obvious grossness of the communicative construct—which is good as the enemy is not desired at the race war planning table—the target group is immunized from this visceral skepticism by the truth that precedes the rant. For, just as Hitler's Germany had been screwed by virtually every nation that mattered, so have the people that Umar appeals to in his abrasive way.

Doctor Umar Johnson is, to the student of human behavior, a nascent gem of striving humanity; the quivering vocal cord of the militant primate determined to grab the world by its throat and defy the existing order. He is the story of Man's Ascent writ small.

Contradictions within the Film

The base contradiction comes at the beginning when the cast is slowly introduced and the case is made that a sure sign that black Americans are oppressed is the fact that they have traditionally been relegated to entertainment roles. Meanwhile the astute viewer sees that nearly half of the expert commentators—who all would have been intellectuals if this were a mainstream Anglo-American effort—are rappers and comedians! I am not complaining, as the two comedians were among the most insightful and considered commentators—my favorite being Dick Gregory—and the two rappers were necessary draws for the young viewer. The filmmaker should have at least called attention to this dichotomy and used it to enhance the message.

One of the academics—the one I find oh so appealing as a possible carrier for my superior alien intellect—discusses the enactment of slave killing laws in Virginia. As she misdates a statute at the mid 1700s and claims it was enacted so that white mistresses could beat to death the mixed race children of their savage husbands [a sorrowful thing that often happened] the filmmaker displays a copy of the actual document dated 100 years earlier and enacted during the white slave rebellions that Dick Gregory had just mentioned!

Fibroid tumors [generally thought to be caused by the HPV virus] are blamed on a white conspiracy to shame black women into using toxic hair products that will give them fibroid tumors and diminish their reproductive capacity. No mention is made of the black 19th Century woman who actually invented these products and is, to date, the single most economically successful independent human female, adjusted for inflation, to have walked this lonely planet. Then, later in the film, in the solutions segment, the filmmakers suggest to the viewer that such hair care products should only be bought from blacks! Hello! If it is rotting black wombs why promote it? King Flex Films needs a Himmler on their editorial staff.

The most appalling contradiction in the film is a moral one, as three of the experts extol the type of traditional slavery as practiced in West Africa in the period of American colonial slavery as being socially good and having no psychological trauma associated with it. These people come frighteningly close to endorsing slavery in the general form it took through most of human history, which would be akin to the abuse, exploitation and neglect of foster children in our society. Indeed the very form of slavery that they promote as having been a symptom of a healthy African society is at the root of the forms of modern domestic and sex slavery that they then point to as a purely white invention. One historical source is misrepresented in this segment. However, I must say that I particularly enjoyed the expert panel's charges that Angelina Jolie and Brad Pitt are adopting children of color so that she will not have to do the housework and Brad will have a sex slave! We all know that Angelina cannot afford a domestic servant and Brad just can't seem to get laid!

Most of the contradictions stemmed from the documentary film methods used without the aid of a fact-checker on the editorial staff. For instance, even as multiple commentators noted that 'all' inventions originated with non-whites, and that white Europeans invented nothing, the narrator informs the viewer that Thomas Edison [who was quite a scumbag invention pirate and manipulative louse] put his name on the inventions and innovations of his black engineering staff, the filmmaker presents a picture of a bleacher full of Edison's white engineers, who, like Carver and Tesla, fell victim to Edison's profiteering schemes.

Even after discussing the plight of Native Americans at the hands of Europeans and some tales of cultural intercourse between black escaped slaves and natives, Umar Johnson goes on to state that blacks are the 'original Americans' and the 'only people with a true claim to this land' [I might have misquoted a little. Forgive me as I was dazzled by the man's beaming eyes.], having somehow overlooked the inconvenient fact that the whites had not managed to wipe out every red person on the continent.

Points of Agreement between Black and White Separatists

The following are those points of agreement I detected between these admitted black separatists and the many white separatists I have known, read, and listened to from this seat of inquisitive verve:

1. That blacks are genetically incapable of being non-violent in non-tropical climates once summer comes around. As one commentator said, 'In the summer we come to our senses...the African in us comes to the surface!'

2. That Mexican and other Latino immigrants are a scourge upon America.

3. That black on black crime is an economic boon to the American ruling class.

4. That Italians are their own special reviled race that neither deserves the 'minority rights' due African Americans or status as full white Europeans.

5. That the other colored races currently flocking to America are all parasites who are just exploiting the civil rights gains earned by African Americans.

6. That Jews are a tribe of sneaky white men who are not to be trusted, but should be emulated as much as possible.

7. That liberal whites are the real enemy of any people who seek to foster a tribal identity and preserve their heritage.

8. That black Africans should not be permitted to gain access to the United States and take advantage of current government policies.

9. That a secret society of white bankers has been pulling the strings behind the world scene for two centuries now, and have decided that the only real use to be made of post agricultural black Americans is as a threat to working class whites.

10. And finally, my favorite, that boxing is a test of racial superiority, and that black men have ruled the ring as the collective racial heavyweight champion since Apollo Creed beat up Rocky Balboa in the 1970s, despite the obvious evidence in the form of an Eastern European lock on the higher weight classes for the last decade.

11. Doctor Umar Johnson does deserve an honorable mention for claiming that the Japanese are white!

Into the Setting Face of Your Dwarf Star

The last agreement between white and black supremacists, that boxing is a test of racial superiority and is also the province of the black American, would appear to be borne out by media coverage, which astutely avoids any mention of the giant white men of recent European extraction who have all but driven black American heavyweights into professional bowling. Thanks to the media obsession with the ghost of Mohamed Ali Floyd Mayweather, a welterweight boxer, who has preserved his unbeaten record by avoiding a fight with a Filipino lightweight, is the number one earner and symbol of modern boxing.

All of you black and white separatist might wish to consider that this impression is maintained by a largely liberal white Jewish boxing press and promotional cadre, who maintain a fascination with pitting fighters together along racial lines, as this increases ticket sales. If, as so many throughout history have contended, boxing is a test of the character of a man and by extension his tribe, what are the lessons to be learned as we consider the drama of heavyweight boxing over the course of the last Century?

Truth is besides the point here. All that matters is the impression. When the first black heavyweight champion Jack Johnson reined, every victory of his saw at least one black man lynched for cheering. It might be said that Johnson had more black blood on his hands than any KKK executioner.

The recent swing to the domination of the heavier weight classes by whites of recent European origin points to boxing as a cultural vector, not a genetic one. You see, Jack Johnson, and the man that the filmmakers marked as his successor, Mohamed Ali, where both taught their craft and guided in their enterprise by white men, who had hitherto dominated that sport.

Now, view the films of Wladamir Klitchsko, Ukrainian Czar of the boxing ring, and you shall see black men working his corner. View footage of 'Krusher' Kovalev, the Russian KO machine, and look to his corner. You will see an African American man who formally ruled his own corner of the light heavyweight boxing world serving as the mastermind.

You see humans even amongst animals such as you culture is the vector to watch. Genetics might catch your eye, shinny baubles of visible evolution that they are. But you, in whatever you do, even if you leave no genetic imprint, such as Nikola Tesla, leave a behavioral thread, a blueprint for action, that will outlive any ape, any ape family, and any ape tribe that perceives their actions to stem from a mindless call within from the magic spirits inhabiting their blood.

A Selfish Postscript

As a way to serve my own need to propagate and also in my guise as a writer to return to the film Hidden Colors 3, I would like to make plain my preference for the light skin lady scholar who sat rather straight—whose name slips me as I was concentrating on her more obvious qualities—an academic who collects data on current 'covered up' lynchings in the American South. While she was waxing genetic about attractive and intelligent slaves of old being selected by their white masters as a 'breeder' [of an accounting staff I suppose], it occurred to me that I am aging rapidly and need to replace myself.

I have, for ages, replicated as a member of the dominant human strain—hence my affinity for Chinese cuisine—and, since your current world leader is a half-breed Euro-African, I do seek shamelessly to imbed myself in the ruling class once again. I will learn this lady's name and research her preferences before recommending myself, and hopefully gaining access to her incubatory precincts. I am sensitive you know, and am somewhat worried as to her opinion of dating eight appendaged extraterrestrials. I did note her preference for men with 'muscles on muscles' when she was describing the qualities of some police officers with a reproductive light in her sparkling eyes.

So earthly brothers, help me out here. If I come across with the following line, will I be overplaying my many hands: "I know Baby the eight appendages can seem off-putting. Yet consider, my sweet little Boo that only two of them are for walking."

Take Me To Your Breeder

Or, should I just present myself in black sunshades and beret to Mister Nasheed, and intone in my best Barry White, "Take me to your Breeder"?

Letter to the Fourlegs

Stone Age people often referred to the mammal population as the four-legs, people as the two-legs and to birds and things that swim as members of separate spiritual 'nations'. If I were an extraterrestrial shaman come to earth three million years ago, and had the ability to speak to the four-legs and knew what I know now about people I would say this:

"Look guys I know you hyenas and lions have your war, and everybody hates the damned leopards, and the dogs are just a pain in the ass and you can't trust the crocs... But seriously, those tree-climbers—and you need to pass this down to your young—if you ever see one of those two-legged monstrosities climb down out of the trees and it picks up a stick or stone, kill him. Then you need to make a deal with the leopards to clear the trees of all of his blood relatives, because that fixation with sharp rocks might just be hereditary.

"And another thing, if you see the apes making nice with the canines, lookout! Okay, laugh if you will. But if you all let the apes and the canines team up, it's all over. This place won't even be safe for me. I'll probably have to scratch seminar appearances after that point. You've been warned."

Just remember, that when we write horror, we are reflecting a dark light from a very deep pool in our collective soul.